CLEANING NATURE NATURALLY

Cleaning Nature Naturally

Kathlyn Gay

WALKER AND COMPANY

NEW YORK

First published in the United States of America in 1991
by Walker Publishing Company, Inc.

Published simultaneously in Canada by Thomas Allen & Son
Canada, Limited, Markham, Ontario

Library of Congress Cataloging-in-Publication Data
Gay, Kathlyn.
    Cleaning nature naturally / Kathlyn Gay.
        p.   cm.
    Includes bibliographical references and index.
    Summary: Discusses old and new methods of
controlling pests and interacting with nature in an
environmentally sensitive way.
    ISBN 0-8027-8118-7 (trade)
    ISBN 0-8027-8119-5 (rein)
    1. Pests—Biological control.   2. Natural pesticides.
3. Environmental biotechnology.   4. Pesticides—
Environmental aspects.   5. Pesticides—Health aspects.
[1. Pests—Biological control.   2. Natural pesticides.
3. Pesticides—Environmental aspects.]   I. Title.
SB975.G39   1991
632'.96—dc20   91-2681
                    CIP
                    AC

Printed in the United States of America

10 9 8 7 6 5 4 3 2 1

Contents

1. Working with Nature

A farmer releases "good bugs" that will attack "bad bugs" in a corn field.

A student builds a bat house to protect bats that eat and control some yard insects.

A lawn-care professional sprays a preparation of tiny soil worms on a golf course to kill insect pests on one of the greens.

A researcher develops plants that will resist disease and insects.

A laboratory technician grows "fancy fungi"—fungal spores that will live and feed on crop pests.

A scientist grows buckets of bacteria that will gobble up harmful wastes in soils and water.

What do all of these people have in common? They are using or developing biological methods to clean up wastes and to control crop, garden, yard, or household pests. They are, in effect, saying "bug off!" to wastes and pests

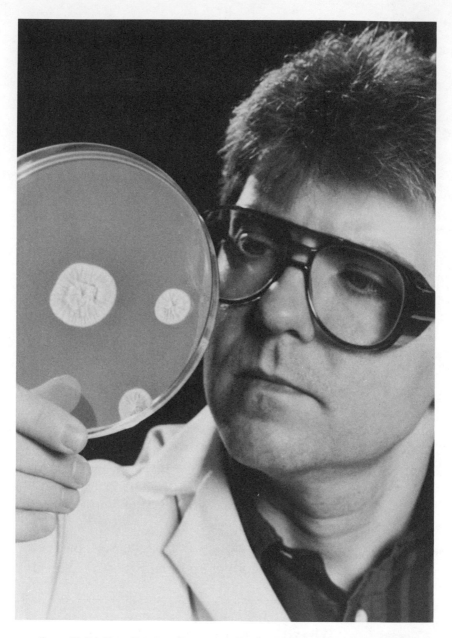

Geneticist Timothy Leathers examines the growth of fungi that may be used to develop a natural insecticide to destroy crop pests. The soil fungi produce enzymes, which in turn can dissolve an insect's shell, or exoskeleton, allowing a fungus to enter and kill the pest. (Photo courtesy Agricultural Research Service, USDA.)

and are finding ways to work with nature to accomplish their tasks.

Most people know that wastes are leftover or throwaway materials. They can be generated from a variety of activities and include household garbage and trash as well as diverse materials from manufacturing, agriculture, and other industries. Many types of wastes contain toxic, or poisonous, substances. But wastes can be broken down by natural organisms and become useful parts of the earth again.

Pests, on the other hand, are more difficult to define and categorize. They include a variety of animals, plants, and microorganisms that are not inherently pests—they all have their particular roles to play in nature. But they are labeled pests (or "bad" or harmful) because they disrupt or endanger people's lives or damage property or are just nuisances.

WHAT ARE PESTS?

Ever since humans first evolved on earth, they probably have had to deal with living things they considered pesky. You might even know some people whom you could call pests, and you might want to tell them to "bug off!" because they are bothering you.

Insects also can be bothersome, and many insects are regarded as pests. No doubt you are familiar with the pesky mosquito. One buzzes menacingly around your head and nosedives to strike your neck. Another zaps you on the arm, and a third gets you on the ankle. You swat, flail your arms, and swat some more as you try to fight off these insects.

The mosquito, however, is only one of hundreds of thousands of different varieties of insects, most of which have been on the planet for millions of years. The majority of insects are small six-legged animals that have wings, antennae, and segmented bodies.

Sometimes insects are called bugs. Even entomologists, scientists who study insects, may use the term "bugs" informally to refer to insects or to such microorganisms as bacteria. However, in the study of insects, scientists divide these animals into orders, with members of each order sharing similar characteristics. Bugs technically belong to the order of insects that includes water bugs, stinkbugs, and bedbugs.

Most people think of bugs and other insects as pests that have to be eliminated or at best tolerated. But entomologist Howard Evans points out that "the virtues and attractions of insects are rarely discussed. By and large, the nuisances and dangers posed by insects are grossly exaggerated." (Evans 1985)

Over 99 percent of all insects are beneficial to life on earth. Consider the lowly ant. Perhaps you think of ants as intolerable pests, especially when they swarm over your food on a picnic table or make a long trail from outdoors to your kitchen counter. Some ants such as carpenter ants may damage buildings by eating out wooden areas. Other species can sting or bite. But of the estimated 12,000 to 14,000 different ant species, most have beneficial characteristics, including the ability to control pests. As entomologists Helga and William Olkowski explain:

> *Regardless of the damage they produce directly or indirectly, it is important to recognize that the same ant species that can be pests are also . . . likely to kill and eat any insect they can find such as flea and fly larvae, bedbugs . . . and termites. [An ant] also aerates the soil outdoors and recycles dead animal and vegetable materials. From that point of view,*

A spinned soldier bug (one of the "good bugs") feeds on a "bad bug," the Mexican bean beetle larva, which devastates snap beans and soybeans. (Photo courtesy Agricultural Research Service, USDA.)

ants provide an ecological cleansing and fertilization service of considerable importance. (Olkowski and Olkowski 1990)

Another kind of organism that people sometimes regard as a pest is mold, a type of fungus. When mold appears on foods, those foods may no longer be edible. Other types of fungi, such as mildew and rusts, destroy grains, and thus are considered harmful pests. Yet, like insects, not all fungi are harmful. Yeast, for instance, is a fungus used in bread making.

Bacteria, which include a wide variety of single-celled organisms, also are considered pests at times. Some bacteria may cause plants to rot or foods to spoil, which can lead to severe poisoning. Others cause a variety of diseases. However, most bacteria are beneficial. For example, some break down dead plants and animals so that the decomposed materials will once again be useful to the environment. Others help change nitrogen gas into a form that plants and animals can use.

If you have ever stepped on a thistle or pricked yourself on a cactus, you know that some plants also can be pesky—they cause injuries. Some plants are considered pests because they are poisonous to people and animals. Others threaten crops. Unless some weeds are controlled, they also choke out range grasses that cattle and other animals use for food. But people have also learned to use some weeds as habitats for insects that control pests. So like insects, fungi, and bacteria, plants can be both beneficial and harmful to humans.

CONTROLLING PESTS AND WASTES

For the past fifty years, many pests that attack animals and plants have been controlled with synthetic chemicals—those developed in laboratories, as opposed to those that occur naturally in the environment and in foods. (Since the term *"synthetic chemicals"* is cumbersome, it will be shortened to simply *"chemicals"* to facilitate reading.)

Chemicals are used to make millions of pounds of pesticides each year. Pesticides include a variety of products, many of which are designed to destroy specific pests. Frequently, they are categorized according to their use. For example, insecticides kill insects; herbicides destroy weeds; fungicides eliminate plant diseases and molds; rodenticides kill rats and mice; and nematicides kill harmful nematodes, tiny soil worms that destroy crops.

Certainly, chemical pesticides (as well as chemical fertilizers) have helped U.S. farmers increase their crop production almost every year over the past half-century. Pesticides also have reduced and even eliminated some dangerous diseases carried by insects and rodents. In addition, a variety of chemicals have been used to preserve fruits and vegetables, preventing food poisoning because of spoilage.

The heavy use of chemicals in agriculture and in other industries, as well as in home and garden products, has begun to backfire, however. Some toxic pesticide residues remain on foods. Some pesticides and fertilizers stay in soils and seep into groundwater, poisoning drinking water supplies. Household pesticides and other consumer products made with toxic chemicals have caused illnesses, some of them life threatening.

Because of the dangers posed by toxic chemicals, many people from all walks of life are trying to reduce these materials in our environment. They are applying techniques that include:

- encouraging beneficial insects, bacteria, and other organisms to reduce or destroy pests;
- disrupting the behavior of pests so they will not reproduce or develop;
- utilizing farming, gardening, landscaping, and forestry methods that discourage pests and reduce toxic wastes;
- using living organisms to clean up pesticide wastes and other toxic materials;
- developing plants and animals that resist pests and disease.

These and other techniques are what this book is about. Some of the methods are new, but others are based on practices used centuries ago.

2. Biological Pest Controls

The place is an ancient Chinese village. The people are farmers from neighboring areas. The action is centered in a marketplace, around a vendor with bags woven from rushes. Inside the vendor's rush bags are nests. Yellow ants made the nests by binding leaves and twigs together with silky threads.

Long ago, Chinese fruit growers attached the nests of yellow ants to the branches of citrus trees, letting the ants swarm over leaves and fruit. The ants captured insects that fed on the oranges.

Over many centuries, Chinese growers found they could help the ants move from tree to tree in the groves. They made bridges of bamboo poles between the trees. As the ants traveled and took up residence in new trees, they formed nests and continued hunting for insect pests. Eventually, the ants created widespread colonies throughout the groves, protecting most of the trees and their fruit.

Today, a practice such as this would be called biological pest control, or biocontrol. Simply defined, biocontrol is a method for manipulating or using natural biological organisms to reduce or destroy harmful insects, fungi, weeds, or other organisms.

One of the most important facets of biocontrol is utilizing pests' natural enemies, which agricultural experts refer to as bioagents. Some of those bioagents are beneficial insects, sometimes dubbed "good bugs." They attack harmful insects, sometimes called "bad bugs." Other bioagents include bacteria and fungi. Nematodes, or microscopic soil worms, may also be bioagents. Although some nematodes are harmful and destroy crops, other strains of nematodes are beneficial and attack insect pests.

PREDATORS, PARASITES, AND PATHOGENS

In biological pest control, bioagents are divided into three categories: predators, parasites, and pathogens. Each type of bioagent attacks pests in its own way.

Predators prey on other organisms. Some predators are fairly large animals like anteaters, which feed on ants and termites. Others are smaller animals such as toads, birds, or bats, which eat insects. Still others may be insects that feed on other insects. For example, pirate bugs eat the eggs and small larvae (the wormlike or caterpillar stage of insects) of moths and beetles that feed on grain products.

One well-known, beneficial insect predator is the lady beetle, better known as the ladybug in the United States (or as the ladybird beetle in Great Britain). There are several hundred species of lady beetles in the United States, but the most widely known are the reddish-orange or tan beetles with black-spotted bodies. Both the larval and adult ladybugs attack a variety of pests, primarily aphids, or plant lice. As soon as larvae emerge from their eggs, they begin feeding on aphids, devouring forty per hour, and in the adult stage continue feasting on plant pests. (Yepsen, Jr. 1984) Some lady beetles eat cottony-cushion scale, tiny insects with a covering that looks like cotton. The scale insects live on fruit trees and suck out juices, literally "sapping" a tree's strength.

Another predator is the praying mantis. People are intrigued by this insect with its delicate-looking body and what appear to be slender "arms" raised as a person would in prayer. But those seemingly fragile arms have sharp spines that can hold another insect in a tight grip before

The seven-spotted lady beetle has cruised a leaf on an alfalfa plant and captured an aphid—a crop pest—which the lady beetle quickly devours for its dinner. (Photo courtesy Agricultural Research Service, USDA.)

devouring it. The praying mantis feeds on a variety of crop pests, including aphids, grasshoppers, and crickets as well as common flies that pester people, pets, and farm animals.

Parasites live on or in other organisms called hosts, from which they draw nutrients. A host could be an insect or other animal, or a plant such as a weed. In biocontrol, beneficial parasites are released into fields and orchards to feed on crop pests, eventually killing them.

In Southern California, beneficial insect parasites are being used to fight whiteflies that have swarmed over ash and other shade trees and fruit trees. Although the whiteflies do not damage fruit, they destroy foliage by sucking juices from leaves, sometimes stripping a tree. They also secrete a sticky substance that coats sidewalks, outdoor furniture, and cars.

Since the whitefly is not native to California, entomologists had to find its natural enemy, which turned out to be a tiny, stingless wasp common in Israel and Italy. California entomologists imported some wasps and then raised thousands of them, which they released to do their pest control work in five Southern California areas.

Another parasitic wasp is being put to work in California avocado groves, where it attacks loopers, insects that eat avocado leaves and fruit. Some avocado growers put out hundreds of thousands of wasp eggs in their groves. Newly hatched wasps look for looper eggs, inside of which they lay their own eggs. After the next generation of wasps hatches, the larvae in turn feed on the looper eggs, killing them.

One parasitic wasp known by the scientific name *Microplitis* may turn out to be a very valuable bioagent. Over the past few years, scientists have been working in several U.S. Department of Agriculture (USDA) facilities across the

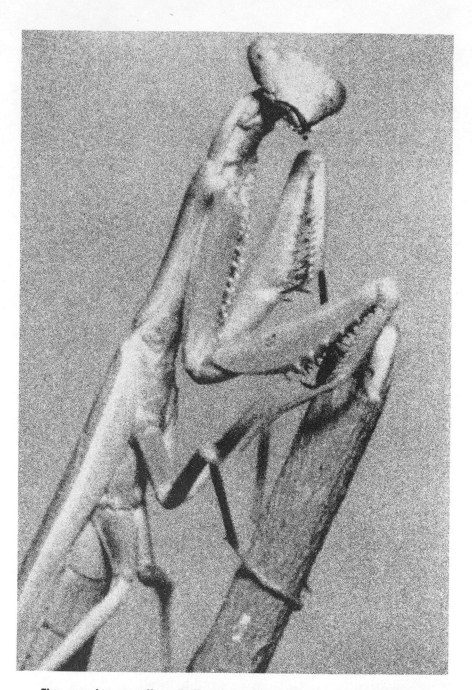

The praying mantis gets its common name from the position it takes while waiting for its prey. This predator feeds on a variety of insect pests. (Photo courtesy M. M. Maedgen, Jr., Biofac, Inc.)

country, raising the wasp to control various species of *Heliothis* insects that are a national menace. *Heliothis* larvae damage $1 billion worth of crops such as cotton, corn, soybeans, tomatoes, and tobacco annually, even though at least $250 million worth of pesticides have been applied to the crops each year. To test the effectiveness of the parasitic wasp, scientists have released five hundred to a thousand female wasps per acre over fields in such states as Texas and Florida. Female wasps have laid their eggs in the *Heliothis* larvae, destroying over 95 percent of the pests on the test crops.

Other beneficial parasites include a fungus that attacks the onion maggot fly, an insect that has a field day in the Great Lakes states, where there are many onion patches. Just one maggot can bore its way through two dozen onion plants within a day. But a fungus can attach itself to a maggot, draining the pest of energy and killing it.

Several strains of nematodes also are beneficial parasites. They attack such pests as root weevils, fire ants, grubs, and termites. Scientists have known for years that parasitic nematodes make excellent bioagents. But to control some types of ground pests, several *billion* nematodes per acre are needed. Researchers had to develop methods to grow huge quantities of nematodes and also had to find ways to preserve and distribute them.

BIOSYS, a California company that is a major supplier of pest control preparations, markets a preparation containing nematodes that are alive but in what is described as a sleeplike state. When the preparation is mixed with water and applied to the soil, the nematodes become activated and search for breeding sites—insect larvae. Adult nematodes enter an insect larva and release bacteria, which attack only the target pest. Bacteria kill the larva within twenty-four to forty-eight hours. The off-

It is only one-half inch long, but this reddish brown wasp can stop the damaging pest *Heliothis verescens,* the tobacco budworm, one of the worst crop pests in the United States. The wasp lays her eggs in the budworm, destroying it. USDA scientists are rearing the wasp to use in biocontrol of other crop pests that are members of the genus *Heliothis* and cause billions of dollars in damage to such crops as cotton, corn, and soybeans. (Photo courtesy Agricultural Research Service, USDA.)

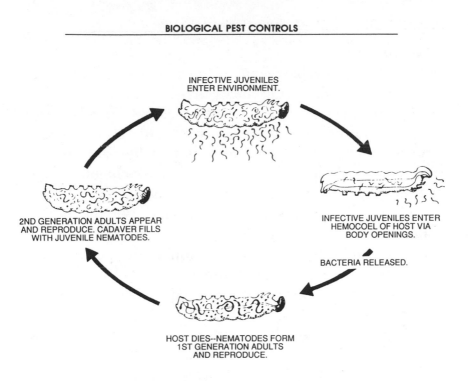

INFECTIVE JUVENILES
ENTER ENVIRONMENT.

INFECTIVE JUVENILES ENTER
HEMOCOEL OF HOST VIA
BODY OPENINGS.

BACTERIA RELEASED.

2ND GENERATION ADULTS APPEAR
AND REPRODUCE. CADAVER FILLS
WITH JUVENILE NEMATODES.

HOST DIES--NEMATODES FORM
1ST GENERATION ADULTS
AND REPRODUCE.

The diagram shows the life cycle of parasitic nematodes that infect, then destroy the larvae of harmful insect pests. (Courtesy BIOSYS, Inc.)

spring of the adult nematodes leave the host to look for other insect larvae and repeat the process.

Pathogens are agents that cause disease and include bacteria, viruses, fungi, and nematodes. For example, a fungus may be injected into soil to cause disease in grubs and beetles that eat plants. Another method is to use disease-causing bacteria to control strains of harmful nematodes, soil worms that destroy crops as opposed to nematodes that serve as bioagents. Pathogens also can cause diseases in weeds. One type controls weeds that would otherwise choke out western range grasses upon which cattle feed.

PHEROMONES

Along with using bioagents, some growers control insect pests with chemical substances that lure insects to traps. Although farmers since ancient times have used diverse lures to capture and destroy insect pests, growers today use substances called pheromones that literally turn an insect's biology against it. Pheromones are chemical compounds that animals, including insects, secrete to communicate with others of their species. When emitted, pheromone compounds may mark an animal's territory or signal danger. Some pheromones are perfumelike compounds released to attract mates.

Scientists are able to make synthetic insect pheromones in the laboratory. Growers bait traps with the substances and sometimes use the traps to capture male insects, which are then sterilized and released. When the insects find females and mate, no offspring are produced, so the insect pests die out.

In other instances growers spray pheromones on a crop to confuse and distract insects; as a result, they cannot find mates and do not reproduce. Cotton growers, for example, may fog fields with a pheromone that disrupts the mating of the bollworm, a pest that destroys cotton plants worldwide.

Since the mid-1980s, entomologists in Byron, Georgia, and Gainesville, Florida, have been researching and developing synthetic pheromones to control two species of peach tree borers and their larvae. The borers feast on the limbs, trunk, and roots of a tree and are pests in areas east of the Mississippi River and in Canada. To control the insects, researchers hang a pheromone dispenser or trap in a peach tree. The pheromone bait, which has been produced in the laboratory, is stronger than the pheromone actually released by female insects to attract males.

Researchers working for a USDA-ARS laboratory place phero-mone traps in peach trees. Pests called peach tree borers are attracted to the pheromone bait inside the traps and caught. Researchers count the number of borers in each trap, which helps determine the effectiveness of this type of biological pest management. (Photo courtesy Agricultural Research Service, USDA.)

As an entomologist explains, "The insects try to mate daily, from around eleven in the morning until about two in the afternoon. This goes on for about two weeks, the lifespan of the adult. Well, when the male futilely approaches the dispenser so many times, he becomes totally confused and exhausted." (Sanchez 1989)

What is the end result? The synthesized pheromones prevent mating and reduce populations of the pests. Those females that remain in orchards are barren, which breaks the reproduction cycle of laying eggs, hatching larvae, and developing adult insects.

OTHER BIOCONTROL TECHNIQUES

A variety of other traps and mechanical devices also are used to control pests. Some are simple devices, such as wood or metal barriers around plants, which gardeners use to deter crawling insects. Ditches and troughs may be used to prevent some insects (crickets, for example) from migrating in droves to farm crops.

One of the mechanical means incorporated in biocontrol of pests on farms is the giant vacuum machine. The Sukup Company in Sheffield, Iowa, a farm equipment manufacturer, worked with several major universities to develop its Bug Beater, which can suck insects off row crops such as strawberries, squash, lettuce, okra, tomatoes, and grapes. Manufactured in several shapes and sizes, the

Some farmers use giant vacuums such as this Bug Beater to suck pesky insects off plants. (Photo courtesy Sukup Manufacturing Company.)

machine can be attached to a tractor. As it travels over rows of crops, fan blades rotate, creating a vacuum that sucks insects inside. With the centrifugal force of the air flow, the insects are smashed against the fan housing, pulverized, and ejected out of the machine.

Bug Beaters have been used primarily by growers in Florida and California. According to a company representative, the machines have been able to remove insects from crops at a rate equal to or exceeding the rate achieved with chemicals. As a result, some strawberry growers have increased yields by as much as 50 percent. (Phone interview and correspondence, August 1990).

Another important biocontrol technique is effective management of the growing environment, often called cultural control. Effective management techniques include rotating crops, scheduling the planting and harvesting of crops to avoid insect damage, plowing land to destroy soil pests, and generally using sound farming practices.

Farmers who rotate crops might vary the kinds of crops grown in a field, planting part of the land in corn, perhaps, and another part in soybeans. Another form of crop rotation is to alter crops on an annual basis or by the growing season. For example, corn might be planted in a field one year, then soybeans in the same field the next year, then oats the following year, and finally alfalfa; the rotation is repeated over the next four years. The process helps prevent harmful insects from gaining a foothold. A soil parasite, for example, might attack a single crop, but if the crop is not planted every year, the parasites will lie dormant for a time. This allows beneficial insects a chance to develop and gain the upper hand so that they can do their pest control work.

Another effective management technique is to study

the behavior of pests in order to control them. For example, rather than applying chemical pesticides that may bring immediate results but also kill beneficial organisms, farmers might grow plants just for the pests. In the Midwest, some farmers plant grasses along a corn field to attract cutworm moths, preventing them from feeding on cornstalks.

Scientists at the University of California, Santa Cruz, have been studying a weed that Mexican farmers traditionally grow along with their corn to protect it. The weed's roots secrete toxins lethal to fungi and nematodes that destroy corn. By trimming the weeds periodically so that they do not crowd out the corn plants or sap nutrients from the soil, the Mexican farmers have been able to control pests that threaten their crops. U.S. researchers have had good results with a similar weed in the United States, according to a report in *Science News*. ("Cultivating Weeds for Pest Control" 1990)

One more management technique is to grow plants that attract beneficial insects, which in turn will attack harmful ones. Paul Buxman, a farmer in Dinuba, California, plants ground cover between his fruit trees and grapevines to make a home for beneficial insects. He also plants poppies near his vineyard. The flowers may be pretty to look at but they have a lethal purpose. They manufacture a toxin that kills off nematodes that otherwise would damage grapevines.

Certain weeds also protect crops. In Weslaco, Texas, agricultural researchers are experimenting with ragweeds and pigweeds that protect bell pepper plants from the leaf miner insect, which at times has destroyed up to 30 percent of the pepper harvest in south Texas. The weeds act as decoys, luring the leaf miner insect away from the pepper plants.

CONTROLLING WEEDS

In spite of the beneficial aspects of some types of weeds, most are considered pests, perhaps some of the worst. Weeds can literally take over a field, garden, or yard. You can see this on vacant lots that are not maintained. An abandoned road or parking lot can be covered in a relatively short time by weeds that work their way through cracks in cement and asphalt.

Ever since agriculture began thousands of years ago, people have had to fight weeds that grow faster than the food crops they are trying to raise. Weeds also choke out range grasses that cattle eat and sometimes injure or poison food animals.

To control weeds, many growers and ranchers use chemical herbicides, or weedkillers. About two-thirds of all pesticides used in the United States are herbicides. They account for about 20 percent of a farmer's input costs (that is, the costs of seed, fertilizer, and other materials needed for farming). Thus, researchers in universities, USDA laboratories, and industries are trying to find less expensive, biological alternatives to chemical weed killers. (Board on Agriculture of the National Research Council 1989)

Many of the biocontrol methods used to protect fruits, vegetables, and grains from harmful insects and disease-causing organisms can be used against weeds. For example, in one biological control project during the 1940s, scientists enlisted the help of a beetle to control Klamath-weed, a plant poisonous to cattle. Great numbers of cattle died after eating the weed.

The Klamathweed probably came to North America with European settlers who brought crops to the New World. Once established, the weed spread across rangeland from Northern California to southern British Columbia.

Scientists from the University of California and the USDA searched Europe for a natural enemy of the weed. They found just the right one—an insect now called the Klamathweed beetle. It was introduced into the western United States, and within ten years it had done its job, devouring 99 percent of the tall weed. The USDA estimates that the beetle saved cattle ranchers $23 million per year. To show their appreciation, ranchers in Eureka, California, put up a monument to honor their beneficial bug.

More recently, scientists have been trying to find bio-control methods to deal with a persistent weed called leafy spurge. No one knows where the weed actually originated or how and when the pest made its way to American soil. But apparently the weed was not accompanied by natural predators, parasites, or pathogens to keep it in check. Today, the pest infests at least 2.5 million acres of grasslands in the northern Great Plains of the United States. It is also a major pest on Canadian rangelands. Cattle refuse to eat leafy spurge and turn their noses up at grasses growing among the pesky weeds.

Ranchers have to spray vast rangelands with herbicides, and usually have to pay $100 an acre or more to control the pest. But the weed can resist herbicides because of its deep root system. Some leafy spurge plants send roots down fifteen feet below the surface soil. One frustrated rancher gave up on herbicides and used propane torches to burn off the spurge on his land, controlling it for five years. But the rancher eventually lost the battle. The weeds grew back, stronger and spreading more rapidly than ever.

Because leafy spurge is such a persistent pest, agricul-

Weed pests called leafy spurge infest at least 2.5 million acres of pasture and grazing lands and farmland in the northern Great Plains of the United States, crowding out desirable plants and causing up to $30 million in agricultural losses each year. But the one-eighth-inch-long flea beetle, shown here, feeds on the leafy spurge and is being tested as a biological control agent to help combat the weed pest. (Photo courtesy Agricultural Research Service, USDA.)

tural researchers have traveled to a number of European and Asian countries where the weed grows but is controlled by its natural enemies. Researchers have found a virtual army of bioagents, including beetles and a fungus from China's Inner Mongolia and other insects from Europe, and have imported them to the United States. Scientists are testing the insects and fungus for their effectiveness and safety before they are released for biocontrol work.

Many weeds (as well as insect pests) in North America probably originated in other countries. Therefore, most of the insects or other bioagents used to control weeds have come from the weeds' native lands. U.S. researchers frequently work with their counterparts in such European nations as Italy, Greece, and France, and in Latin America and Asia to find the bioagents needed. An example is the work of botanist Charles Turner in Albany, California, who is experimenting with biocontrol of the star thistle, a weed with needle-sharp spines. The plant grows one to three feet high in fields across the western states. Its sharp spines can injure livestock when they eat it, and like other pesky weeds it crowds out plants that animals could eat.

Turner learned that the weed is a native of Greece, so he contacted scientists at a research station in Thessaloniki. The station is part of a worldwide network of facilities operated by the Agricultural Research Service (ARS) of the U.S. Department of Agriculture. Experiments in the ARS Greek laboratory showed that the weed had a natural enemy: a peacock fly. A single fly larva can tunnel into and eat more than 90 percent of the seeds in a star thistle flower, preventing the weed from reproducing.

After lengthy tests to show that the fly would not become a crop or animal pest and was safe to bring into the United States, Turner imported hundreds of the flies

Scientists are seeking to use natural predators to control plant pests like the thistle plants described in the text and the musk thistle, shown here. In the photograph, an entomologist at the Agricultural Research Service Laboratory in Rome, Italy, collects beetles from thistle plants. The beetles are natural enemies of the thistle plants and eat the plant, destroying it. (Photo courtesy Agricultural Research Service, USDA.)

from the Greek laboratory. With the permission of federal, state, and county agricultural agencies in the United States, he released the flies in California fields that were full of star thistles. If the flies adapt well to their new environment, they could produce enough offspring to clear fields of the prickly, pesky weed.

Another species of parasitic fly was imported from Europe to control knapweed. This pest also infests rangelands. The tiny imported flies lay their eggs in the knapweed seed heads. After the eggs hatch, the fly larvae feed on the seeds, disrupting their development.

Additional beneficial insects are being imported to control aquatic weeds in states like Florida. Such weeds as hydrilla, water hyacinth, and alligatorweed grow rapidly and clog streams and irrigation systems in the state. The weeds also consume oxygen, which endangers other aquatic life. But insects such as the hydrilla weevil and others that feed on specific plants serve as tiny weed whackers, eating their way through leaves and stems and clearing waterways.

In spite of many efforts to control weeds with beneficial organisms, weeds still plague croplands, rangelands, and gardens. So researchers in laboratories at a variety of locations across the United States are experimenting with other ways to work with nature to control weeds. For example, plant scientists are conducting laboratory tests on alfalfa to see how a component of the plant can be used as a weed killer. Scientists also have isolated a toxin called medicarpin that alfalfa produces. They believe the toxin helps alfalfa ward off insect and fungi attacks and competition from weeds. What scientists want to learn is how much medicarpin different varieties of alfalfa produce and whether the toxin could be used as a bioherbicide, or a weed killer made from natural organisms.

A weed-hungry flea beetle feasts on alligatorweed, which has clogged waterways in such states as Florida. By using the flea beetle as a biocontrol agent, alligatorweed has been almost eliminated from Florida waterways. (Photo courtesy Agricultural Research Service, USDA.)

Would you believe that sweet potatoes also release substances that can suppress weeds? Scientists in Charleston, South Carolina, have been able to extract natural chemicals called phenolics from the skin of sweet potatoes. In laboratory tests, the chemicals curbed the growth of eight varieties of weeds.

Such laboratory research could lead to the development of a variety of bioherbicides. It also contributes to the technology that is being used to produce plants with high levels of naturally occurring toxins. In fact, weed research is just one of many agricultural projects designed to develop ways to protect crops without using chemicals that endanger the environment and public health.

3. Biocontrol Versus Chemical Control

Even though various methods of biological pest control have been used successfully for more than one hundred years in the United States, they have gone in and out of favor. When biocontrol was first introduced during the 1800s, some American growers were desperate for solutions to a major pest problem. The cottony-cushion scale threatened to destroy citrus trees in California. At that time, chemical pesticides were not widely available, and most growers and farmers depended on natural pest control agents. So USDA researchers began an urgent search to find bioagents that would control the citrus pests.

Scientists determined that cottony-cushion scale had been brought into the United States from Australia, which is where researchers went to find a natural enemy of the parasite. That enemy turned out to be the vedalia beetle, or ladybug. Researchers collected Australian ladybugs, brought them to California, and then let them loose in the citrus groves. The ladybugs quickly multiplied and gobbled

More than one hundred years ago, vedalia beetles (better known as ladybugs) like the one shown here were released in California to feed on cottony-cushion scale that damaged citrus crops. (Photo courtesy Agricultural Research Service, USDA.)

up cottony-cushion scale, almost purging the groves of the life-sucking pests.

In other early attempts to use biological pest controls, U.S. scientists visited China in 1915 to study the citrus groves that were being managed in much the same way as in ancient times, using ants as bioagents. The U.S. researchers wanted to find ways to protect Florida orange crops. Like the California citrus crops, the Florida oranges were being destroyed by pests. But after observing the ant colonies in the Chinese citrus groves, the American scientists mistakenly concluded that the ants were ineffective in pest control. They also noted that even though the ants attacked insects that were damaging citrus, the ants brought other parasites such as mealybugs with them.

Mealybugs are scale insects—they have scaly shells and cluster on trees or plants and suck out juices, sometimes killing off their hosts. The citrus ants protect mealybugs just as other types of ants protect aphids. These insects are like an ant colony's dairy herd. Ants "milk" the mealybugs, stroking them so that they discharge a nectar called honeydew that the ants lap up for food.

In later studies, American scientists found that the mealybugs in the Chinese citrus groves were controlled by parasitic wasps. In addition, there was an abundance of predators. Lady beetles and lacewing larvae apparently helped control the scale insects.

THE ARRIVAL OF CHEMICALS

Since about the 1930s, biocontrol methods have been used in the United States to reduce or destroy many pests that damage field crops such as corn and wheat. Pests that are harmful to fruits and vegetables ranging from apples to zucchini also have been controlled. According to the Agricultural Research Service of the USDA, growers now are able to control at least fifty major insect pests and eight to ten weed pests by using bioagents.

Although biocontrol of pests is receiving increasing attention today, that was not the case after World War II. During the 1940s, DDT was discovered. DDT's tongue-twisting name is dichloro-diphenyl-trichloroethane. It is a mixture of chlorine, benzene, and alcohol.

DDT was used in the armed forces to kill disease-carrying body lice. The chemical also killed mosquitoes that carried life-threatening diseases such as malaria and yellow fever. The pesticide was so successful in getting rid of dangerous pests that it was called a miracle chemical. After the war, there was widespread pressure in the United States and some European countries to manufacture DDT pesticides for home and agricultural use. They were, in fact, manufactured and used on a grand scale.

However, many scientists were concerned about the effects of these poisons on people and the environment. Why? Because they learned that once DDT is applied, it has the ability to stick around in the environment and remain toxic for weeks or months. It also can be transported easily by water or through the air. In fact, DDT has been found in soil and water samples taken from areas far from where the pesticide was used originally.

Scientists also discovered that DDT accumulates in the food chain. For example, DDT may be absorbed by plants, which are then eaten by birds and other wildlife. Although some of the DDT is excreted, the rest remains in tissues and continues to build up. Seals and birds with high amounts of DDT in their bodies have been found in the Antarctic, where no such chemical has been used.

In 1962, a book called *Silent Spring* by Rachel Carson alerted the public to the dangers of DDT and similar pesticides. Ten years later DDT was banned in the United States. By that time, however, huge amounts of pesticides had been and were being applied in attempts to control pests on farms and ranches, and in vineyards, orchards, and home gardens.

AN ONSLAUGHT OF CHEMICALS

Pesticide use continued to increase over the next two to three decades. Because weeds and insects began to resist pesticides, more and more toxins were needed to control them. Still, pests caused damage, as much or more than they did before pesticides were applied. In some cases, pesticide spraying led to increases in crop pests.

For example, from the 1950s through the 1970s, the USDA sprayed potent chemical pesticides over millions of acres in efforts to control fire ants that damaged crops grown in southern states. The spraying programs eventually were stopped after the pesticides were found to be carcinogenic (cancer causing). Officials also found that the pesticides killed many of the fire ants' predators.

With their natural enemies gone, the ants were able to multiply and travel widely, setting up their mound homes across the southern part of the nation. Today, fire ants have spread across 250 million acres in eleven southern states, with no long-term solutions in sight to eradicate them.

Other insect pests also have multiplied after prolonged pesticide use. Consider the effects of pesticides on corn crops. According to the USDA, American farmers seldom used pesticides on the corn they grew forty-five or fifty years ago, but insects destroyed only 3.5 percent of the nation's corn crop each year. During the 1980s, however, insects damaged 12 percent of the corn annually even though the use of pesticides had increased at least a thousand times! (McDermott 1990)

As U.S. farmers applied more and more pesticides, they also increased the use of chemical fertilizers. A number of factors contributed to these increases. In the first place, most growers followed the advice of agricultural researchers at universities and USDA facilities. Over the years, the experts tested and recommended use of both chemical pesticides and chemical fertilizers. At the same time, manufacturers of pesticides and fertilizers developed the kinds of products that agricultural experts recommended. Growers, in turn, used the products and saw results—increased production.

Agrichemical usage also increased because many farmers switched from growing diverse crops to growing a single crop on a massive scale, a practice called monoculture. Since the 1950s, farms have become huge food "factories," specializing in raising one type of crop. Between 40 and 45 percent of the total U.S. corn crop is grown this way today. The practice is so well established that it is now known as traditional or conventional agriculture.

Monoculture has been encouraged by some U.S. agricultural programs. For example, the federal commodity

Nearly half of the corn—a major crop in the United States—is grown on a massive scale, planted year after year in an agricultural practice called monoculture. (Photo courtesy Kansas Department of Commerce, Travel and Tourism Development.)

program, supported by federal tax dollars, provides subsidies, or payments, to farmers who specialize in growing only one or two of the major crops, such as corn, soybeans, wheat, rice, or cotton. The amount of payment a farmer receives depends on the number of acres planted and the yield per acre. Naturally, a farmer wants the best yield possible. Thus, excessive amounts of agrichemicals may be used to push production of a single crop year after year.

Yet single-crop farming may deplete nutrients from the soil. For example, if a farmer plants corn in a field each year, the crop will use up the nitrogen (a nutrient plants need) in the soil, requiring the use of more and more nitrogen fertilizer. But if a farmer plants alfalfa, for example, or soybeans every second or third year, the crop will replace nitrogen used by the corn.

Another factor contributing to greater reliance on agrichemicals is the way farmers pay for the costs of farming. At the beginning of a growing season, many farmers must borrow money to buy seed and other supplies. But banks frequently require that growers show they use agrichemicals as a precondition for getting the loan. Some insurance companies also refuse to insure against crop losses if fertilizers and pesticides are not used.

Even farmers who do not take part in federal subsidy programs and do not practice monoculture may overuse agrichemicals, particularly pesticides. Michael Smith, a young farmer in Michigan, said that many farmers in the area where he lives believe they *must* use pesticides.

Smith explained that on his family farm "we used to have a lot of problems in the corn fields, as many farmers do, with corn borers and earworms that destroy the crop. For twenty or thirty years while my father farmed this land, we used tremendous amounts of pesticides year after year. That seemed to be the only way to get rid of pests. But one spring after my wife and I took over the farm, I went out into a field that had just been sprayed. I saw a lot of robins flying sideways. Some fell over on the ground, and others were dead. They'd been poisoned."

Although the dead and damaged birds made Smith wonder about the dangers of pesticides, not until a later planting season did he decide to change farming practices: "Our two oldest boys—they were two and five at the time—were out playing in the fields after we'd planted corn. I thought: Hey, they can't do that—there are poisons out there. I felt it was really crazy to keep dumping poisons all around us every single year. Now I rotate—change the type of crops I plant in a field each year. I was surprised how easy that works. By moving our crops around year after year, the pests don't have a chance to get established. Now we don't use any pesticides at all." (Interview, August 1990)

DEBATING THE EFFECTS OF CHEMICALS

Most farmers who plant and harvest huge amounts of crops do not follow Smith's farming practices. But an increasing number of Americans, including agricultural groups, entomologists, environmentalists, and government leaders, are calling attention to the excessive use of pesticides. As Cornell University entomologist David Pimentel points out, "Of the approximately 500 million kg of pesticides applied in the United States, often less than 0.1 percent of those applied to crops actually reaches target pests." (Pimentel and Levitan 1986)

What happens to the pesticides that fail to reach their targets? Some remain in the soil and may be taken up by plants or stay on the surface of plants. Although insects harmful to the plants are destroyed, beneficial parasites and predators are killed also.

During irrigation or after a rainfall, pesticides (along with fertilizers) in the soil may run off into nearby streams or seep into groundwater. Although many people think of groundwater as a kind of underground river, such is not the case. Rather this source of water saturates the earth below the surface, somewhat the way water soaks into a sponge. Contaminants that move through the soil may take years to reach a groundwater source, and once

Water from irrigation often runs off into streams or seeps into groundwater, carrying with it chemical pesticide residue that can contaminate water supplies and present health hazards. Because of the health dangers posed by chemical pesticides, many individuals and groups want to see increased use of biological pest controls in agriculture. (Photo courtesy U.S. Geological Survey.)

polluted, the groundwater may be contaminated for decades or even centuries.

Nearly half of the U.S. population depends on groundwater for drinking water. The EPA has found at least seventy-seven different pesticides in underground water supplies of thirty-nine states. These pesticides include aldicarb, known to be highly toxic to laboratory animals; DBCP (1,2-dibromo-3-chloropropane), which may cause kidney, liver, and lung damage and is a probable carcinogen; and EDB (ethylene dibromide), which also can damage internal organs and lead to cancer. These, along with several dozen other pesticides, have since been banned or restricted in their use, but they still contaminate drinking water.

Over the past few years more than a dozen studies in several countries, including the United States and Canada, have connected Parkinson's disease, a nerve disorder that causes tremors, with exposure to pesticides in well water. A recent study of three hundred people in Kansas shows that those in the group who have lived in farming communities and have consumed well water most of their lives are twice as likely as nonfarm residents in the group to suffer from Parkinson's. According to the Kansas study and others, farmers and pesticide workers are at the greatest risk, although not all people continually exposed to pesticides will suffer from the disease. Scientists do not yet know why some people are more susceptible than others.

Pesticides are a particular hazard to migrant farm workers—people who travel, usually from southern states through northern states and from one agricultural field to another—during growing seasons to plant and harvest crops. Farm workers frequently are exposed to toxins while working in fields treated with pesticides or during aerial sprayings of pesticides. Although few long-term studies have been done to document health problems of migrant workers, many suffer nerve damage and other chronic illnesses from pesticide exposure, according to a report in the *Journal of the American Medical Association.* (Goldsmith 1989)

Consumers also may be at risk from pesticides, particularly if toxic residues from the chemicals remain on fruits and vegetables. The U.S. Food and Drug Administration (FDA) monitors food for pesticide residues and says that its "sampling and testing show that pesticide residues in foods do not pose a health hazard." (Farley 1988) But between sixty and seventy pesticides that legally can be used on foods are suspected carcinogens.

In 1989, the Natural Resources Defense Council (NRDC), an activist group that conducts scientific studies on environmental problems, released a report of a two-year study indicating that over six thousand preschool children faced cancer risks because of pesticide residues on foods they eat. A recent NRDC publication explains that

children consume proportionally more fruits and vegetables—and therefore more pesticides—than adults do. Children don't actually eat more food then their parents, in absolute terms, but relative to their body-weight . . . they consume more of most foods than adults. Produce makes up about one third of the average child's diet, and the typical preschooler's diet is dominated by fruits, which are the foods most *likely to be contaminated by pesticide residues. (Garland 1989)*

Since children consume large amounts of apples and apple juice, the NRDC in its report emphasized the health hazards of apples treated with Alar, a trade name for a chemical called daminozide used to enhance the color and growth of apples. Once the NRDC report was released, many consumers across the country refused to buy apples and apple products treated with Alar. Some growers quit using Alar, and some food processors would no longer use apples sprayed with Alar. At the same time a number of supermarket chains across the United States announced that they not only would refuse to sell Alar-treated apples but also would test other produce for pesticide residues and post the results for customers.

However, the U.S. Environmental Protection Agency (EPA), which as its name implies is supposed to protect citizens from environmental hazards, said that its studies showed the health threats from Alar had been exaggerated. Some health officials argued that the major health risk in American diets is not pesticides but too much fat. In addition, medical experts pointed out that health risks from human activities (such as smoking) are much greater than from pesticide residues on foods.

Other health experts say that fears over pesticide residues are unjustified because the public is more at risk from bacteria and parasites that occur naturally in food. Salmonella bacteria, for example, frequently have been found in eggs and poultry and can cause poisoning if not destroyed by sufficient cooking. A variety of molds that occur in stored foods may be toxic, and hazardous chemicals are produced naturally during fermentation of such foods as yogurt.

Bruce Ames, a biochemist at the University of California, supports this view. In fact, he and his colleagues have developed a method by which the toxic effects of a substance can be measured. Although Ames's methods and theories are being debated in the scientific community, the biochemist has appeared on TV talk shows to tell the public that "99.99 percent of all pesticide carcinogens now ingested by humans are natural" and can be found in such items as herb teas, mushrooms, and various fruits and vegetables. The message clearly is that since people are not getting cancer from "natural carcinogens" in foods, then why worry about synthetic chemicals? (Brookes 1990)

Ames's views have been quoted frequently by the National Agricultural Chemical Association and a group called the American Council on Science and Health, which is supported by agrichemical industries. The council produced a film that presents Ames's theories and uses the film to counteract consumer and environmental groups that argue against synthetic pesticide use.

Consumers Union (CU), an independent organization that tests consumer products, takes issue with the methods Ames uses for determining cancer risks. CU noted in its magazine *Consumer Reports* that some natural toxins, such as those found in peanut butter and natural root beer, *are* strictly regulated. The magazine feature also points out that pesticide residues "are in foods because someone made an economic decision to use those chemicals. Those whose businesses prosper from the use of pesticides usually assert that the benefits of use outweigh the risks." In CU's judgment, the hazard index developed by Ames is based on examples and assumptions that "are wrong or debatable . . . [thus] the conclusions are suspect." ("Too Much Fuss About Pesticides?" 1989)

LEGAL ACTIONS

The federal Insecticide, Fungicide, and Rodenticide Act (FIFRA) of 1972 was designed to protect the environment and public health from the harmful effects of pesticides. In 1988, the act was amended to require that the EPA conduct tests on six hundred ingredients in some fifty thousand pesticide products. The agency must then set the tolerance level for the maximum amount of a pesticide considered safe to leave on agricultural products. But most tolerance tests have been conducted for new pesticides, not for the approximately four hundred on the market before the 1972 law went into effect. Congress mandated that the EPA review both old and new pesticides by 1997, an impossible task, since testing a single pesticide usually requires years of study.

Environmental and consumer groups have criticized the law, calling it "FIFRA-lite." The law does not address the issue of pesticides in groundwater. Nor does FIFRA contain provisions to protect farm workers who apply pesticides or work in groves or fields containing heavy pesticide residues. Critics also were displeased that the act did not include regulations to control the export of pesticides that have been banned in the United States.

However, in mid-1990, a major agricultural bill was passed that included an amendment to FIFRA prohibiting the export of banned pesticides. Congressional leaders hope the legislation will break what has been called a circle of poison. Until the new law became effective, banned pesticides were sent to other nations to grow food products, some of which were later imported and sold in the United States.

In addition, recent legislation prohibits the use of ethylene bisdithiocarbanate (EBDC) used in fungicides, products designed to control fungal diseases that damage fruits and vegetables, ranging from apples to watermelons and potatoes to tomatoes. A National Toxicology Program study released in 1989 showed that the risk of cancer and birth defects from EBDC exposure is much higher than what the EPA considers safe. After application, the EBDC breaks down and forms a potent cancer-causing substance. Even before the ban on this fungicide, several major manufacturers of EBDC products, including Du-Pont, announced that they would no longer recommend the use of EBDC fungicides on most of the fifty-five vegetables and fruits to which it has been applied.

Because of the growing public concern that fungicides, herbicides, and insecticides may endanger our health, many state and local governments have passed their own pesticide regulations, which frequently are tougher than federal laws. Within the past few years, most of the midwestern states and California, Oregon, and Florida have passed laws restricting the amount of pesticides and fertilizers in groundwater. If there is contamination, the cost of cleaning up the groundwater may be prohibitive, so regulators usually require source reduction—cutting down the amount of pesticides being applied. To many environmentalists source reduction is the only way to go. John O'Connor, the director and founder of the National Toxics Campaign, which helps communities organize to fight polluters at the neighborhood level, writes:

> *Twenty years of environmental laws have been a miserable failure because our regulatory approaches don't touch or challenge production—the products and processes of industry, agriculture and transportation. Even the strictest enforcement of the laws simply means an ever-increasing amount of poisons being permitted in our environment. Government "manages" pollution into the environment, but never stops it at its source. (O'Connor 1990)*

Whenever regulations on agrichemicals are proposed, protests are heard from manufacturers, growers, and food processors. They believe that reducing pesticide use would force the cost of production up and increase the prices for food products. Some growers argue that strict controls and higher prices would put them at a disadvantage when trying to compete with food produced in nations or states where there are less stringent regulations.

Although some growers are reducing the amount of pesticides they use, the vast majority depend on some pesticides and fertilizers to grow food and fiber crops. Herman Delvo, a USDA statistical analyst, notes that "farmers will change their practices when it is feasible and profitable to do so. Researchers at agricultural universities must continue to test and demonstrate successful alternative farming methods. Then, private industry must manufacture environmentally safe agricultural products. After that farmers probably will be able to grow crops on a large scale with reduced amounts of chemicals. But it will take years to bring about all of these changes." (Telephone interview, October 1990)

4. Growing Crops the "Natural" Way

While scientists, manufacturers, farmers, consumers, and others argue the pros and cons of agrichemicals, some individuals have been growing foods and ornamental plants the "natural" or "organic" way. Many people say that since organic means carbon-containing, *all* agriculture is organic. But organic growing refers to farming and gardening *without* synthetic chemical fertilizers and pesticides, which of course was the way agriculture and gardening were practiced before the advent of such chemicals..

Some of the most well-known organic growers are those at the Rodale Farm in Emmaus, Pennsylvania. The founders of the Rodale experimental farm also established a publishing company that over the decades has been producing magazines and books with information about organic gardening and farming.

Until recently, the Rodale growers and their supporters were looked on as oddities, "bucking the trend of the times toward chemical growing," wrote Robert Rodale, who directed the Rodale operations until his death in late 1990. He pointed out:

> *The scientists who were against us always looked at only part of the garden challenge. They were soil experts, or plant disease specialists, or they knew plenty about poisoning troublesome insects with chemicals. They believed in dividing the garden into compartments like that was the only scientific way to think and act. We organic people always looked at the whole garden as a living system—a more scientific way to think of something as complex as a garden. I argued that we were the true scientists.*
>
> *Now our view is prevailing . . . . We have been welcomed into the mainstream of gardening and farming. No longer are we shunted into a corner and labeled the extremist fringe . . . . (Rodale 1989)*

Indeed, there are signs that some organic growing methods are once again becoming an accepted part of agriculture. Even farmers who do not use purely organic methods (that is, they may apply some chemicals) may attempt to increase farm production without depleting natural resources or damaging the environment. They are applying methods that are alternatives to traditional farming practices. These methods are known as sustainable or alternative agriculture or by such terms as low-input or biological agriculture.

WHY SUSTAINABLE AGRICULTURE?

An estimated 5 percent of the nation's 2.1 million farmers are engaged in sustainable or alternative agricultural practices. Why? One of the most important reasons is the need to sustain high levels of agricultural productivity in the United States. Some farmers and agricultural research scientists believe that soil erosion, water pollution, depletion of water resources, and other agricultural and environmental problems are threatening to undermine crop production in the nation. Unstable crop production can lead to food shortages and economic difficulties. Applying ever-larger amounts of chemicals to boost production simply adds to the problems.

From all parts of the country and the world come reports from growers who describe applying pesticides only to find pests returning to their fields. Growers may

The management staff at the Necessary Trading Company, a mail-order firm that provides products for sustainable agriculture, continually tests methods and products that are effective and safe for the environment. Here staff member Chuck Chandler tills under a legume that adds nitrogen and organic matter to soil in the research garden at company headquarters in New Castle, Virginia. (Photo courtesy Necessary Trading Company.)

spray several times without results. Each spraying of course adds to production costs. Worldwide, more than $20 billion is spent annually to control just insect pests that damage crops.

Another reason that growers turn to sustainable agriculture is their concern about health hazards. Along with chemical pesticides, the heavy use of chemical fertilizers has contaminated some groundwater supplies. Nitrate chemical compounds from fertilizers and decomposing animal wastes seep through the soil. Although soils naturally contain low levels of nitrates from the breakdown of organic matter (that is, matter containing the element carbon), high levels of nitrates become pollutants in well water used for drinking. Nitrates in drinking water can cause a reaction in infants that cuts off oxygen to the brain, leading to a condition known as blue-baby syndrome. Nitrates may also be responsible for some cancers.

Exposure to herbicides—weed killers—also can cause health problems. When farm workers are exposed to herbicides for more than twenty days per year, their cancer risk is six times greater than for nonfarm workers, according to the National Cancer Institute. Acute pesticide exposure also can result in poisoning that leads to serious illnesses and sometimes death. (Board on Agriculture of the Natural Research Council 1989)

Some farmers turn to sustainable agriculture because they believe in being stewards of the earth—they are committed to the land. But over the years, croplands have deteriorated. In many parts of the United States and in other countries the soil has been overused and abused. Monoculture—single-crop farming—not only has depleted nutrients in the top layer of soil (called topsoil), but also has caused erosion. Topsoil, which takes thousands of years to build up, has blown or washed away because there is not enough organic matter to hold it in place.

If you dig a hole several feet deep, you may be able to see the difference between the topsoil and the subsoil, the soil underneath. Although the colors of soils in the United States vary from very dark brown to reddish and cream-colored, topsoil is usually a darker shade than the subsoil because it contains more decayed organic material—plant and animal matter. Microscopic organisms such as bacteria, fungi, and protozoa break down plant and animal wastes, changing them into nutrients that plants can use. The lighter shades of the subsoil usually indicate that some of the organic matter has been lost, used up by growing plants.

Soil scientists writing for *Scientific American* explain that "soil is not just another instrument of crop production, like pesticides, fertilizers, or tractors. Rather it is a complex, living, fragile medium that must be protected and nurtured to ensure its long-term productivity and stability. . . . Healthy soil is a hospitable world for growth. Air circulates through it freely, and it retains moisture long after a rain." (Reganold, Papendick, and Parr 1990)

To promote healthy soil, growers who engage in sustainable agriculture have to spend time learning "how the soil works," notes Leland Eikermann, president of the Farm Alliance of Rural Missouri. He advises farmers to use practices he has found successful, such as rotating crops, planting cover crops to supply nitrogen, and planting windbreaks (trees or other vegetation). "Windbreaks more than pay for the space they take up by protecting crops . . . thereby increasing yields," he writes. (Eikermann 1990)

Eikermann points out that farmers will turn to sustainable agriculture when they see that reducing chemicals does not also mean reducing their crop yields. In a recent experiment in Illinois, for example, twelve farmers compared their production on land farmed by conventional methods with plots farmed using sustainable techniques. Eight of the twelve Illinois farmers have been able to maintain or improve crop yields on their demonstration plots. Such results help convince other growers to try the alternative approach. (Gunset 1990)

A recent two-year study on alternatives to conventional farming practices also has prompted some farmers to change their farming methods. The study was conducted by the Board of Agriculture of the National Academy of Sciences (NAS), and findings were released in 1989. In its four-hundred-page report, NAS concluded that farmers who practice sustainable farming methods often have productive and profitable operations, even though these farms receive little financial help from federal agricultural programs. The NAS recommended wider adoption of proven sustainable systems, "fundamental reforms in [federal] agricultural programs and policies" with more economic incentives for growers using sustainable methods. The result, NAS said, would be "significant benefits for farmers, the economy, and the environment." (Board on Agriculture of the National Research Council 1989)

INTEGRATED PEST MANAGEMENT

One of the most important aspects of sustainable agriculture is manipulating crops to outwit pests. It is part of a strategy known as Integrated Pest Management (IPM). Practitioners of IPM deal with an individual farm field (or home garden) as a system and determine the best way to control pests without disrupting that system. This means finding the relationship between pests and their natural

At a USDA biological control laboratory in Niles, Michigan, an entomologist checks out some of the beneficial insects that are raised in the facility. Millions of lady beetles are among the beneficials produced. The ladybugs feed on aphids (also grown at the lab) and are kept in cold storage until ready to use as predators, gobbling up "bad bugs" that damage crops. (Photo by the author.)

enemies, monitoring to see whether pests are increasing to the point where they will damage plants, and using chemical intervention only when absolutely necessary to prevent economic losses. About 8 percent of U.S. farmland is being managed with various IPM strategies. (Board on Agriculture of the National Research Council 1989)

Although chemicals may be used in an IPM strategy, they are usually applied only as a last resort and not as is now recommended for conventional farming methods. In conventional applications, growers use pesticides on a regular schedule during a season—perhaps spraying up to six times—regardless of whether pests are endangering crops. As a result, beneficial insects are destroyed along with harmful ones, and new pests (dubbed superbugs or superpests) that resist pesticides come along to take over.

One crop that has received a lot of attention from IPM practitioners is cotton. Cotton growers long have used pesticides to control what *BioScience* magazine calls "the most insecticide-intensive crop: It [cotton] receives almost half the insecticides used in the United States and now hosts more than 25 resistant [pests] . . . many of which seriously damage cotton only after their natural predators have been subjected to chemical controls." ("Managing Pesticide Resistance" 1985)

However, many cotton growers in Texas and California now use IPM strategies and plant the types of cotton that mature early, before pests have a chance to develop. Growers also place predators and parasites in the fields to destroy such pests as the bollworm and boll weevil. Pest larvae are destroyed after harvest when the remains of the plants are burned.

Some farmers control insects by harvesting before pests can do damage. Missouri farmer Eikermann explains that "instead of applying $25 or $30 worth of

At the Fillmore Insectary in California, black scale, shown here attached to a twig, is produced on oleander plants and then used for raising parasites that will attack the black scale in citrus groves. (Photo by the author.)

insecticide to kill alfalfa weevils, I just use the time-honored tradition of cutting the alfalfa earlier, before the weevils get bad." (Eikermann 1990)

How do farmers or growers determine whether pests are getting "bad"? Some growers, particularly vegetable and fruit growers in states such as Florida and California, hire field scouts to monitor pests. The scouts may be employees of a university biocontrol program or commercial scouting service, or they may be farm workers trained for the job. Scouts gather detailed information about a field such as how the land is fertilized and irrigated. Then they go out into a field several times a week or every day if necessary and literally inspect pests.

After recording information about the types and number of pests they see, field scouts can determine whether there is a problem. If harmful insects or diseases are found, scouts recommend the type of action growers should take, which might be to apply insecticides or fungicides. But usually the dose is much smaller and is applied earlier than would be the case in conventional vegetable growing. Early application of a pesticide may control the pests immediately. The method helps to cut pesticide costs and may prevent contamination of groundwater supplies.

Pest management is also necessary after food products are harvested. Grains, for example, are stored on farms or in grain elevators, huge storage bins that hold grain until it is sold. Large numbers of pests such as granary weevils, rusty grain beetles, lesser grain borers, moths, and mites attack grain before it goes to storage bins and also when it is in storage.

How can grains be protected? Buddy Maedgen can tell you. He and his wife, Loretta, own and operate Biofac Insectary, in Mathis, Texas, where they produce millions of beneficial insects for use in pest control, with particular emphasis on the natural enemies of grain pests. They got started in the business because of problems they were having with pests attacking crops on their own farm. "We used plenty of chemical pesticides but the pests became resistant, so we decided to try bioagents," Buddy Maedgen says.

In 1978, Maedgen built an insectary to produce beneficial insects. The first was a parasite called *Trichogramma.* "That's a miniwasp that lays its eggs in the eggs of many different kinds of pests," Maedgen explains. The developing wasp larvae feed on the eggs of moths that produce

A tiny parasitic wasp called *Lemophagus curtus* injects her eggs into the larva of a cereal leaf beetle, killing the larva before it can mature. This wasp is one of several used in a biological control program to protect cereal crops from pests. (Photo courtesy Agricultural Research Service, USDA.)

such pests as the corn earworm and corn borer. This tiny wasp is harmless to all forms of life except moth eggs. According to Maedgen, it can be used in a variety of settings including home pantries, health food stores, supermarkets, food warehouses, grain storage facilities, gardens, field crops, orchards, and plant nurseries. (Correspondence, July 1990)

During the 1980s, USDA studies showed that beneficial insects such as *Trichogramma* could be used to control pests in stored grains. So Biofac began producing large numbers of tiny wasps plus other beneficial insects and selling them to operators of grain elevators in Texas and Oklahoma. Elevator operators released the insects atop grain bins every two weeks over several months. They reported that parasites and predators reduced grain pests by 95 percent at a cost of one-fourth to one-half of what would be spent on chemical pesticides.

With such success stories the Biofac business should have expanded rapidly. Not so, the Maedgens found out when FDA officials "arrested" a grain bin where Biofac insects were at work. The FDA called the insects food additives and ruled they had to be registered. Later FDA inspectors decided the insects were illegal because they had been placed in the grain by people, in spite of the fact that the use of beneficial insects not only is legal but is advocated by USDA agencies. In addition, regulators were not swayed by arguments that all grain is cleaned before milling.

The insects in effect became illegal aliens, which led to intervention by other federal and state regulators, and the grains were seized by the FDA. Biofac and the owners of the grain appealed to former Texas Agricultural Commissioner Jim Hightower, who long had advocated natural pest controls and sustainable agriculture. But Hightower was unable to obtain even a response from many queries to the FDA. Finally, a news exposé and a March 1990 report on the TV show *60 Minutes* documented what has been called a bureaucratic bungle. The FDA released the grain and informed the Maedgens that they could continue to use and sell bioagents to control pests in stored grain.

IPM IN OTHER NATIONS

Just as IPM methods have become established practices in some areas of the United States, they also have become a part of farming methods in other countries. Why? Because as is true in the United States, farmers in other nations are finding that overuse of chemical pesticides can lead to major agricultural problems. Rice growers in Indonesia know this only too well.

During the early 1900s, Indonesian farmers used intensive farming methods, such as planting improved strains of rice and using fertilizers, which helped the nation of 13,677 islands grow enough grain to feed its 170 million people, a remarkable feat according to most agricultural experts. However, a flying insect called the brown planthopper threatened rice crops during the 1970s. The pest feeds on rice plants and causes them to rot in the field. Since chemical pesticides were being widely used around the world, the Indonesian government encouraged rice farmers to apply dozens of chemical insecticides to control the brown planthopper. The strategy worked for a while. But in the mid-1980s, the destructive planthoppers were back—with a vengeance.

Although some farmers applied insecticides up to twenty times within a six-week period, the insects destroyed hundreds of thousands of tons of rice. Fortunately, earlier studies by entomologist Peter Kenmore of the United Nations Food and Agriculture Organization (FAO) paved the way for salvaging Indonesia's rice crop. Kenmore and other researchers had found that farmers were spraying pesticides regardless of whether pests had infested their fields. As a result, the insecticides were killing off at least a hundred different types of predators, including flies, beetles, wasps, and wolf spiders, which can eat up to twenty brown planthoppers per day. In short, the chemicals poisoned the beneficial insects, leaving the rice fields for the pests to devour.

With the FAO studies at hand, the Indonesian government in 1986 banned the use of fifty-seven pesticides on rice crops and set up a program that will eventually train all of Indonesia's 2.5 million rice farmers in IPM strategies. Led by FAO's Kenmore, teams of scientists trained field workers who in turn trained groups of farmers, who became trainers themselves, spreading the word about IPM. Trained farmers now know how to diagnose problems—for example, to determine whether brown spots in rice fields are because of fungus or poor nutrition or pests.

Farmers also learned to figure the ratio of beneficial insects to pests and how much damage rice plants can take without a loss in yield. As Kenmore explained to a journalist: "Plants can lose half their leaves in the first month of growth without harming the yield, but only 10 percent of the leaves later on." (Vaughan 1988)

With IPM knowledge, Indonesian rice farmers have cut their use of pesticides by almost 10 percent and reduced their costs by more than one half. Only when pests become a threat do farmers spray pesticides. Yet rice yields have remained about the same or have increased slightly. Although chemical companies have complained that the Indonesian government and FAO have exaggerated the planthopper problems, the IPM program has continued. Because of the success of the Indonesian program, the FAO has similar experiments under way in major rice-growing nations such as Bangladesh, Thailand, Malaysia, India, the Philippines, and China.

IPM has been successful with other crops as well. In Taiwan, for example, techniques such as crop rotation and pheromone traps have been used to control sweet potato weevils. The strategy has helped reduce damage to sweet potato roots in one area from 40 percent to less than 1 percent of the crop.

In Peru, IPM came to the aid of cotton growers, who during the 1950s adopted the agricultural practices of the United States—extensive use of chemical pesticides. As in other parts of the world, pests of cotton plants became resistant to pesticides, and superpests developed. Entomologists were able to introduce IPM strategies and save cotton crops.

Scientists in Peru are now working on biocontrol programs to prevent losses in potatoes, a staple food for people in the Andes mountain areas. In spite of wide use of potent pesticides, weevils, moths, nematodes, and a disease called bacterial wilt are a few of the pests that destroy potato crops. Among the strategies that entomologists are developing in laboratories or applying in the fields are the use of

- a fungus that occurs naturally in soils around potato plants and which kills weevil larvae;
- beetles that are natural predators of potato weevils;
- sex pheromone traps that attract male moths, preventing damage to stored potatoes;

- crushed oyster shells in soil to promote the growth of organisms that produce natural antibiotics, which in turn control bacterial diseases;
- dried or powdered leaves of certain plants to cut rot and insect pests that attack stored potatoes.

Insect pests that cause havoc in African nations also are under attack by scientists. Not only do insects damage crops, but some pests such as tsetse flies and mosquitoes threaten human health. Tsetse flies spread a deadly sleeping sickness among farm animals and people, and mosquitoes carry malaria, which is fatal for many African children. But through a research organization called the International Centre of Insect Physiology and Ecology (ICIPE) in Nairobi, Kenya, biocontrol techniques are helping to reduce crop, animal, and human pests.

Directed by Thomas Odhiambo, an entomologist from Kenya, some of the ICIPE projects helped control tsetse flies. Although the flies were controlled somewhat with traps, more widespread and radical methods were needed to clear areas heavily infested with the pests. Some of the measures included "stripping the land of vegetation, killing all the animals on which the fly feeds and bombarding the area from the air with pesticides," according to a report in *Smithsonian* magazine. (Bass 1988)

But the flies were stopped only temporarily, and they began invading treated areas again, so some scientists decided to develop improved traps. They are inexpensive devices made from plastic bags and cloth. But the traps incorporate color and the odor of cow urine or buffalo breath to attract far more tsetse flies than was possible with older traps. The flies die inside the devices.

Controlling crop pests is another effort that is part of the African program. ICIPE scientists have developed natural pathogens such as viruses to kill pests. As in other nations, the African researchers also have introduced disease-causing nematodes into the soil. The nematodes carry bacteria that infect and kill off corn borers, which are a menace to maize plants.

Wherever biocontrols are being applied, they are part of worldwide efforts to encourage agricultural practices that help farmers meet the needs of an increasing world population. The World Commission on Environment and Development estimates that enough food must be produced to feed an additional eighty million to one hundred million people each year. Most of the population growth is in developing nations, some of which are suffering already from food shortages. But rather than emphasize heavy use of chemicals to increase food production, there is growing understanding around the world that food and fiber must be produced without destroying the environment or depleting natural resources. Usually, this means using pesticides only on targeted pests and encouraging natural enemies to attack insects, disease, rot, and weeds.

5. Using Biotech Tools

The efforts to reduce chemical dependence in agriculture are being boosted by many researchers around the world. In the United States, scientists are working in government research centers, university laboratories, or commercial companies. Many of the researchers are part of a broad field known by the catchall term biotechnology, or biotech as it is called for short.

WHAT'S BIOTECH?

Basically, biotechnology is a collection of tools and techniques that scientists apply to living organisms in order to modify or create other organisms or products, which are used for many diverse purposes. As applied in agriculture, biotech has been hailed as a new practice, but it actually began during ancient times, just as biological control of pests had its start centuries ago.

Early peoples used basic biotechnology when they domesticated animals, taming wild wolves, goats, and horses. They bred new strains of animals that would serve their needs: for example, the ox was developed to pull a plow. Ancient people also domesticated crops like corn and strawberries. Such food crops originated with wild plants that were improved upon by farmers who selected the best seeds for each season's planting. Later, hybrid plants were produced.

Plant hybridization began with the discoveries of an Austrian monk, Gregor Mendel, who in the 1860s was able to crossbreed pea plants to improve the product. Hybrid plants have been an important part of modern agriculture ever since, helping to bring about larger yields of crops to feed ever-larger numbers of people around the world.

Today, agricultural scientists apply modern tools and techniques to enhance natural biological processes. They use these techniques to make changes in food (both plant and animal) products at a much more rapid pace than was possible even twenty years ago.

One of the most important techniques in biotechnology is transferring characteristics or traits of one organism to another, a highly complex process called genetic engineering. In the process, genetic material of living cells is altered to produce new substances or to perform new functions.

Genetic engineering became possible in recent years as scientists gained deeper understanding of a molecule called DNA, which is part of the chromosome structure of cells and carries coded instructions called genes. The instructions contained in the genes determine the characteristics, or traits, of all living things. To transfer traits from one organism to another, scientists use a variety of techniques. One makes use of enzymes—natural substances "that work like chemical scissors and glue . . . to snip genes out of DNA molecules and stick them into the

DNA of microbes," explains the Industrial Biotechnology Association. The microbes with transplanted genes may be inserted into the cells of plants, which then will have the traits of the new genes and pass those traits on to the next generation. (Industrial Biotechnology Association, *Biotechnology at Work,* 1989)

BIOPESTICIDES

Gene transfer and other biotech tools are helping scientists develop a variety of biological products and methods, many of which are being or will be used in agriculture, home gardening, lawn care, and forestry. Some of those products are biopesticides, or pesticides that are made from biological materials rather than synthetic chemicals.

For example, dozens of U.S. biotech companies have for years been using strains of *Bacillus thuringiensis*, a soil bacterium, to prepare biopesticides. The bacterium, known as *Bt* for short, produces a toxin that causes an insect's stomach cells to rupture, starving it by making it unable to digest food.

Most *Bt* pesticides are target specific, that is, designed for specific pests. Scientists must first isolate a strain of *Bt* and identify the toxin it contains. Some toxins may be poisonous to pests such as the gypsy moth, others may be poisonous to mosquitoes, or caterpillars, or beetles. However, because the *Bt* toxin is targeted for a specific pest, it does not kill beneficial insects, and it is harmless to humans and other vertebrates and to plants.

Recently, the Mycogen Corporation, a California company established in the 1980s specifically to manufacture biopesticides as alternatives to chemical pesticides, genetically engineered a *Bt* product that kills harmful nematodes. Using the techniques developed to produce the

Geneticist Phyllis Martin is testing a new bacillus (*Bt*) solution—a biological pesticide—on tomato plants. The tests will help determine whether this biological control is effective on such pests as the Colorado potato beetle. (Photo courtesy Agricultural Research Service, USDA.)

biopesticides, the company expects to engineer plants that will resist nematodes.

Another firm, Igene Biotechnology in Columbia, Maryland, began in 1988 to market a different type of biopesticide that also destroys soil nematodes. The product is made from crab shells and other shellfish wastes. Within the wastes is a protein that encourages microorganisms in the soil to produce enzymes. The enzymes will in turn attack the kinds of nematodes that destroy about $5 billion worth of vegetable, fruit, and grain crops every year.

Other kinds of biopesticides are under investigation. At the Northern Regional Research Center in Peoria, Illinois, for example, scientists Timothy Leathers and Subhash Gupta have identified a soil fungus that produces enzymes capable of dissolving an insect's shell. The fungus can then enter the insect and kill it.

According to Gupta, genes that make the enzymes could be placed into other fungi, which would then grow on insects that they otherwise would not infect. Gupta and Leathers say the fungi could be used to develop a fast-acting bioinsecticide.

In another research effort, scientists at a Columbia, Missouri, laboratory have found that a tiny parasitic wasp injects caterpillars with crystallike substances that destroy caterpillars and thus prevent insects from emerging. In laboratory tests, the crystals from the wasps have stopped the growth of such crop pests as bollworms, cabbage loopers, and asparagus beetles in their caterpillar stage. Scientists hope to identify the toxic chemical in the crystal, which could lead to the production of another biopesticide.

In similar work in Albany, California, scientists have found that petunias carry natural chemicals that could be used to destroy tomato pests. Toxins taken from the

Microbiologist Subhash Gupta and laboratory technician Kimberly MacDonald examine insect larvae treated with fungi. The fungi produce enzymes that can dissolve an insect's shell, in a similar fashion to the way that detergents dissolve stains from clothes. The fungi then enter the insects and kill them. (Photo courtesy Agricultural Research Service, USDA.)

petunias' leaves and stems were fed to fruit worms that prey on tomato plants. The toxins stunt the growth of fruit worms and kill off their larvae.

HELPING PLANTS RESIST PESTS

Research also is under way to develop antibiotics that will help plants resist pests. One antibiotic comes from a strain of bacterium *Pseudomonas fluroescens*. Scientists say the bacterium is the only known producer of the antibiotic, and it may be able to protect wheat plants from a fungus disease called take-all. The name of the disease actually describes the action of the fungus—it can destroy an entire crop of wheat and affects wheat plants worldwide.

Plant pathologists, scientists who study plant diseases and pathogens, also are working on ways to use beneficial fungi to help plants protect themselves from harmful fungi in topsoil. Scientists have found beneficial molds—fungi—that can be fermented and grown in the laboratory, then combined with gelling agents, formed into pellets, and dried. The pellets, which are nontoxic, break down in the soil, protecting plants from other, destructive molds.

Crop Genetics International, a private company working in cooperation with the USDA's Agriculture Research Service, has developed plants that can fight harmful insects with their own built-in insecticide. The process makes use of two naturally occurring bacteria: *Bt* and another plant-dwelling bacterium called an endophyte. The gene in *Bt* that codes for a toxin is inserted into the endophyte. The altered endophyte then is placed inside a plant, in this case corn, and the *Bt* toxin is produced in stalks, leaves, and roots. Field tests show the toxin cannot spread to the environment because the endophyte cannot live outside the corn plant.

Do plant scientists actually inoculate cornstalks to protect them? Only in the first field tests of this technology. Corn seeds are being modified with the endophytes, and the biopesticide will go to work as the plants grow, protecting corn from such pests as the corn borer, which causes about $500 million in crop damages each year. The altered seed, which is being introduced by DeKalb, a major seed company with headquarters in Illinois, costs more than other seed. But farmers are expected to show higher profits from the genetically engineered corn, since no insecticides will be needed to protect their crops.

THE PROS AND CONS OF BIOTECH

Whatever the benefits of biotechnology, laboratory changes in natural organisms have been the focus of some heated public debates. Some environmentalists are concerned that genetically engineered organisms (GEOs) might disrupt natural balances in the environment. Some critics of biotechnology also worry that laboratory-altered microbes could multiply rapidly and, if they carry disease, destroy the soil or spread disease beyond their targets to other plants and animals. Others have suggested that the release of GEOs could trigger horrible phenomena such as bacteria that would eat up forests or an algae that would cover the oceans.

Some of the concerns stem from a few instances of ecological imbalances that have occurred when "foreign" insects or plants have been introduced into an environment accidentally or have been imported for a purpose. An example is the gypsy moth, which was brought into the United States during the 1800s by a naturalist on the East Coast who hoped to breed the moths to produce silk. When the moths were in the caterpillar stage, some of them escaped from their breeding site and began feeding on leaves of trees. The moths multiplied, infesting the neighborhood, then an entire town, and finally the whole New England region.

Over the years, the gypsy moth has eaten the leaves of hundreds of thousands of birch, oak, and poplar trees and also has damaged fruit trees. It has become a pest primarily because the natural enemies that could have controlled the moth have been killed off by heavy use of chemical pesticides.

Yet transferring an insect or other animal or plant from its original habitat to an alien environment is not the same as genetic engineering, scientists say. An animal or a plant in its native environment usually is kept in balance by its natural enemies; placing it in another, vastly different environment where there are no natural predators or parasites allows it to overpopulate and become a pest.

Genetically engineered bacteria are changed to fit a specific environment. They function for a specific purpose and do not live or multiply outside their target environment, the experts say. The National Academy of Sciences and the vast majority of scientists working in biotechnology say no evidence exists showing that genetically engineered bacteria and other genetically altered organisms have created environmental or human health hazards.

Even as biotech advocates tout the safety and benefits of genetically engineered products, they also know there are some drawbacks. For example, plants may not grow or produce well with too many genetic changes, and if yields drop, a crop loses some of its value to a grower. Even though plants may contain biopesticides, insects frequently develop mutations, or changes in genes, that allow them to survive poisons, passing those mutations on to generation after generation until they are immune to toxins, whether biologically or synthetically produced.

Another major difficulty with genetic engineering is using the technology to attack symptoms rather than basic problems. For instance, some scientists are trying to develop plants that resist chemical pesticides, but developing pest-resistant plants may be more ecologically sound than engineering superplants that are able to withstand the effects of heavy doses of chemicals. (Miller and Ackerman 1990)

REGULATING BIOTECH PRODUCTS

Because so many new biotech agricultural products are ready to be tested or marketed, there have been many different opinions about regulating them. Public interest groups usually argue for strict controls, fearing that new products could be as hazardous to the environment and public health as agrichemicals. Such groups would like to see regulations that require companies to obtain licenses before manufacturing any biotech products. Critics also want companies to demonstrate the safety and effectiveness of organisms and to show how possible harmful effects could be abated.

Biotech proponents argue that federal and state laws already provide strict regulation of biotech products. For example, EPA regulations require acute toxicology tests for products with genetically altered *Bt* bacterium. In other words, before companies can manufacture and sell *Bt* biopesticides, they must demonstrate that test animals exposed to high doses of the products are not harmed. Additional testing, such as for the effects of residues, must show that the products do not poison mammals, aquatic life, birds, and other nontarget organisms such as beneficial insects.

Other federal laws regulate imports of plants and insects that may be used for biological pest control or genetically altered for biocontrol purposes. Researchers must obtain a permit from the USDA to import potential bioagents. The permit is granted if field tests show that the imported organisms are effective bioagents and are not likely to become pests themselves.

Scientists working with genetically altered organisms designed to control pests must also obtain permits for field tests of products. When applying for a permit, a researcher must provide a detailed description of a genetically engineered organism, explain how and where it will be tested, and what control measures will be used.

At present, five or six federal agencies, including the Environmental Protection Agency, the Food and Drug Administration, and the Department of Agriculture, share the responsibility for controlling the use of biotech organisms. As a result, a biotech product may be regulated by two or three agencies. For example, if a company uses genetic engineering to develop a microbial pesticide, the product would be subject to EPA regulations established by the federal Insecticide, Fungicide and Rodenticide Act. The USDA would have to test the biopesticide to determine whether it would damage plants, and the FDA would determine whether the residue levels of the biopesticide met federal safety standards. (Industrial Biotechnology Association, *Answers*)

Because some regulations for biotech products can be conflicting or confusing, representatives of biotech companies have been lobbying Congress, asking for clear federal laws regarding their products. Without distinct federal guidelines, states could decide to set up their own rules for the release of genetically engineered plants and microorganisms. Indeed, more than twenty states are considering some type of legislation to regulate biotech products, and some states have already passed laws regulating genetically engineered organisms.

One such state is North Carolina, which requires that a company or individual apply for a permit to release genetically altered organisms. Professionals in the state's Agriculture Department review the application, but a state public review board also has input. The board includes officials from the North Carolina Biotechnology Center, a state facility to promote biotech industries. Researchers, farmers, representatives of biotech industries, public interest groups, universities, and government also are on the board, which has the responsibility of notifying the public when genetically engineered products are to be released. But no local governments can set up additional regulations for biotech products. (North Carolina Biotechnology Center 1989)

Several biotech firms have publicly stated that they believe the North Carolina law is straightforward and reasonable. Others, however, generally oppose individual state regulations because they can duplicate federal laws and create even more confusion, if not chaos.

U.S. Senator Patrick Leahy, who for years has advocated a national policy on biotechnology, points out that the biotech industry usually follows research procedures stricter than those required by federal or state laws. Leahy notes, however, that "voluntary compliance is not the same as having good regulations. History is full of examples of technology proceeding without an adequate regulatory framework—and then becoming mired in public opposition. Nuclear power is a case in point. . . . Clearly, advice and guidance must come from those individuals and organizations who work in the biotech field every day. Together we can foster an environment where biotechnology will be safely and profitably developed." (Leahy 1988)

6. Waste Eaters

Along with applying biotech tools in attempts to improve crop production without endangering the environment or human health, scientists also are using biological organisms to reduce contaminants such as chemical pesticides and fertilizers in soil and water. Researchers actively search for bacteria and fungi that have adapted and thrived in soil and water contaminated with not only agrichemicals but also such pollutants as oil and toxic wastes from industries. The experts then use biotech tools to encourage the organisms to multiply and to gobble up contaminants. In addition, scientists genetically engineer organisms to attack toxic substances.

SOME FIGHTING FUNGI

At the University of California at Riverside, microbiologist William Frankenberger has been involved since the mid-1980s in experiments to reduce soil contaminants in the Kesterson wildlife refuge located in central California. The contaminated soil is a result of irrigation practices and heavy use of chemical pesticides on farmlands in the state's Central Valley. Over several decades, irrigation water had seeped through the soil or had run off carrying selenium, pesticides, and other chemicals into basins, wetlands, and rivers. Because of high evaporation rates and poor drainage in the wildlife refuge, the hazardous substances concentrated in the area.

Although small amounts of selenium, a trace element in soils and rocks, are essential for life, large amounts are poisonous. The EPA has set a safe standard of selenium in soil at four parts per million (ppm); in water the standard considered safe is ten parts per billion (ppb). But in the Kesterson wildlife refuge, selenium concentrations had reached disastrous levels—250 ppm in soil and 3,000 ppb in water. The selenium killed off thousands of birds. Countless others were born deformed—with curved beaks, for example, or brains poking through eye sockets.

Federal EPA and state officials considered a variety of methods to deal with the problem and finally decided to fill in the contaminated area with tons of "clean dirt," literally covering up the problem. But UC microbiologist Frankenberger and his colleagues have been allowed to work on test sites at Kesterson. The scientists have used naturally abundant fungi in the contaminated soil beneath the fill dirt to transform selenium into harmless compounds. The fungi change selenium into a nontoxic gas. But the fungi work slowly, so the microbiologists accelerate the process by adding carbon, derived from pectin in citrus peelings, a natural by-product from citrus crops grown in California.

In test sites at Kesterson and elsewhere in California, fungi are being "fed" orange and lemon peels, which are worked into the soil. The fungi thrive on the additional carbon and have reduced selenium concentrations about 28 percent each year. (Ferrell 1989)

Some fungi used to attack other toxic substances in soil are being genetically engineered. At Texas A&M University, for example, scientists James Wild and Frank Raushel have been able to engineer an enzyme, called the OPD enzyme, that will break down organophosphates, substances frequently used in agricultural pesticides.

There are many kinds of organophosphates, but most disrupt the nervous system. Some destroy pests on contact and also can poison humans who ingest or inhale vapors or absorb compounds through their skin. Parathion and diazinon are two potent organophosphate pesticides that have caused deaths among farm workers who apply the compounds. Organophosphates concentrated in the soil also are a hazard.

When the Texas A&M scientists built their enzyme, they found a soil bacterium which carries a gene that produces a scavenger enzyme. In the laboratory, Wild and Raushel used other enzymes—molecular scissors—to separate the genetic material producing the enzyme. They modified the gene so that it could be inserted into several types of viruses. Those viruses in turn were inserted into insect cells in order to produce large amounts of the enzyme for research. The enzyme attacks the bonds that hold together molecules of insecticides such as parathion or diazinon and nerve toxins used as chemical warfare agents. If the molecule's internal bonds are broken, the compound degrades, and its toxicity is reduced or lost.

The office of public information at Texas A&M notes that the U.S. Army provided part of the funding for the OPD research, hoping that the enzyme could be used to neutralize the effects of chemical weapons. But the enzyme also has great potential to clean up toxic residues of

Waste-treatment plants like this one are in use throughout the United States to treat sewage. (Courtesy D. R. LeBlanc, U.S. Geological Survey.)

pesticides used in agriculture. (Texas A&M University news release, August 1989)

MUNCHING MICROBES

Other cleansing agents being put to work are bacteria. Sewage treatment plants long have depended on bacteria and other microorganisms to decompose materials in wastewater. Early in the 1900s, engineers who were developing sewage treatment plants for rapidly growing urban areas discovered that bacteria and oxygen help break down some of the contaminants in wastewater. Aeration—continued movement of air through wastewater—became the standard way to activate bacteria in sewage treatment plants.

Much of the solid waste, or garbage, generated worldwide also is controlled by microbes in soil and water. These waste eaters make mincemeat of such materials as food scraps and other organic materials. For example, munching microbes are being used to decompose restaurant garbage. A California company called Bio-Care packages bacteria that help decompose food scraps, grease, and even detergents. The company sells the bacteria by the box for garbage control.

Bacteria are especially important in the management of municipal waste today. As more and more landfills—places where garbage is dumped—are filling up, waste collectors are having trouble finding dumping sites. About one thousand municipal and private waste-processing companies in the United States are turning to an old process: composting garbage and yard wastes, allowing bacteria to decompose the materials. The decomposed material, or compost, then can be used as a nontoxic fertilizer.

Some companies are packaging bacteria for home and industrial use that help decompose various kinds of wastes. The company that makes Septi-Save also makes bacterial products that clean drains and control odors. (Courtesy Bio-Care, Inc.)

However, composting is a long process if bacteria are allowed to work at their own pace. Organic materials might not decompose for months or even years, particularly in areas where bacteria are dormant during cold weather.

In recent years, waste disposal companies have developed ways to turn garbage into compost quickly. One company, the U.S. Waste Group, has developed a bacterial enzyme that transforms ordinary garbage into nutrient-rich compost within three to six weeks. A company executive says, "The resulting compost—a dry material—is packaged and can then be used or marketed by cities to enrich the soil in parks, on farms, lawns, or other areas

Solid waste collected in cities and towns is hauled to landfill sites, where the waste is dumped and covered over with dirt. However, many landfills across the United States are filling up, so some cities are composting garbage and yard waste, turning it into fertilizer. (Photo by the author.)

where soil conditioners are needed." The material also acts as a natural insecticide and absorbs moisture so it helps prevent soil erosion. (Phone interview, December 1988)

OIL-EATING MICROBES
While an army of microbes munches away on garbage or decomposes contaminants in wastewater, other bacteria gobble oil that pollutes soil and water. Usually soil becomes contaminated when petroleum-based products are dumped on land sites or when oil leaks from underground storage tanks.

In some cases, the EPA or another government agency requires companies or individual landowners to clean up oil contaminants because they seep into aquifers and threaten supplies of drinking water. A common and costly treatment method has been to dig up soil and haul it away to a landfill. Soil contaminated with petroleum products usually is considered hazardous waste, and federal laws require that it be placed in a special hazardous waste site.

However, hauling contaminated soil to a waste site does not deal with the basic problem—getting rid of the petroleum. For that reason an army of waste-eating bacteria may be called in to do the job in a process known as bioremediation. In the case of oil contaminants, the process includes putting bacteria to work to decompose hydrocarbons, compounds of hydrogen and carbon that make up petroleum products.

Bob Winn, an expert in bioremediation techniques, has used bacteria to clean up thousands of cubic yards of contaminated soil in northern Indiana. In one project Winn and his crew were called in to clean up a plot of land about the size of half of a football field and three feet deep. The ground, he says, "was so saturated with diesel fuel that you could pick up a handful of dirt and squeeze the oil out. Long before we started treatment of the soil, it had been virtually dead, polluted with over 8,000 parts of hydrocarbons per million parts of soil." Winn and his crew encouraged many munching microbes to gobble up the oil, and after only four weeks, the pollutants had dropped to 49 ppm in the soil.

"I first discovered what actually happens when I worked in Texas," Winn explains. "I was in an area where there had been a diesel spill some five years before, and around the edges of the spill we could see that the fuel was decomposing. The spill area had shrunk, and the soil around it was much richer and healthier. Why? Because bacteria, which exist in soil everywhere, were eating the carbon atoms that link petroleum molecules. When bacteria eat the carbon, they break the bonds and the fuel is changed into something else. That can happen with any organic compound. If left alone, the bacteria would eat away on the fuel spill but it would take hundreds of years for the bacteria to break down the fuel to a harmless biomass."

To decompose organic compounds in a shorter period of time, bacteria need a little help. Munching microbes that are able to adapt to a polluted environment need to be isolated—set aside, as was the case with the treatment that Winn described—and then encouraged to multiply. Meantime, the contaminated soil is excavated and placed on huge vinyl sheets, which protect the ground underneath. Bacteria can then be placed in the contaminated soil.

Nitrogen may be added to create a healthy environment for the bacteria, and the soil is tilled on a regular basis to increase the oxygen, which the bacteria need to survive and multiply. In a few weeks or months, depending on the size of a contaminated area and the type of organic pollutant, the bacteria have decomposed contaminating material and the soil is healthy again.

What happens to the bacteria when they run out of food—do they go somewhere else for a feast? Will they become harmful to the environment or people?

"No way!" says Winn, who has answered these questions many times before. "When bacteria run out of food they become dormant or die off just as they do when it is too cold or there is not enough oxygen for their survival." But the soil they have left behind may be clean enough to eat! As Winn says, "I'm very careful about what I put into my body, and I'd be willing to take a spoonful of dirt that we've treated with bacteria and eat it to show how safe it is."

Although Winn does not eat soil, he was able to show environmental officials that treated soil is healthy. In a simple demonstration, he filled two five-gallon buckets—one with treated soil and the other with "ordinary" soil from a noncontaminated area—and planted bean seeds in both. The plantings received equal amounts of water. "In a month, the beans in the treated soil were twice the size of the beans in the other soil," he says. "The reason is that the treated soil was loaded down with nutrition—what was once diesel fuel became a biomass readily available to plants, and dirt worms and lower organisms that keep soil healthy." (Personal interview, July 1990)

One of the largest bioremediation efforts to clean up oil contaminants is under way along Alaska's coast. In April 1989, the Exxon oil company's tanker *Exxon Valdez* spilled nearly eleven million gallons of crude oil into the bays and inlets. At first, cleanup methods involved everything from trying to contain the spill in the seawater to

The Exxon oil company's tanker *Exxon Valdez* and some of the
oil it spilled in April 1989 during the worst such spill in history. Oil-
eating microbes are useful in helping to clean up such messes.
(Courtesy AP/Wide World.)

spraying hot water on the shores to mopping up oil-slick rocks with absorbent towels. By summer of that year, Exxon and EPA officials decided to stimulate the growth of natural bacteria along the shoreline. They spread nitrogen and phosphorous fertilizers on test plots, and bacteria multiplied and cleaned up the first test plot in ten days. Within a few weeks the munching microbes had lapped up the oil in a larger area. During the winter, the bacteria were dormant. The fertilizing continued in the spring of 1990, and the bugs again got busy on the oil-soaked beaches. Officials expect to repeat the process for several more seasons.

A similar technique was used on floating oil spilled from a Norwegian tanker, the *Mega Borg*. The tanker was damaged in an explosion while in the Gulf of Mexico. Fire following the explosion burned much of the oil, but a forty-acre oil slick spread over the seawater just south of Galveston, Texas. Some Texas officials, fearing ecological damage to the coastline, were reluctant to use bioremediation to clean up the oil. However, the Texas Land Commission decided to call in an Austin biotech company, Alpha Environmental, to use oil-eating microbes on the spill. It was the first time bacteria had been used in the open sea, and several hundred pounds of bacteria in a dried form mixed with cornstarch were sprayed over the spill in the cleanup measure. Within a few weeks, the microbes had done their job, apparently without hurting the environment. (Newspaper reports, June 9–August 1990)

Another use for munching microbes is to let them make a natural coating—called a surfactant—for coastal lands to prevent damage from oil spills offshore. With the help of soil bacteria, Ananda Chakrabarty, a University of Illinois professor, developed the surfactant, a soapy material that he says is nontoxic and would decompose quickly.

How did the bacteria make this coating? It is part of the natural process the microbes use to decompose oily materials that are their regular diet. But the professor speeds up the process by placing large numbers of the bacteria in a fermenting machine; then he extracts the surfactant, purifies it, leaving dead microbes behind. Although the coating material has yet to be field tested, the scientist believes the product could be quickly sprayed on coastal areas to prevent contamination if an oil spill threatens the land and vegetation. (Van 1990)

DETOXING WASTE

Toxic chemical waste is a major challenge for bioremediation experts. Across the United States and around the world, waterways and soils are polluted with hazardous wastes from agriculture and industry. Many of these materials contain a combination of chemicals or heavy metals that microbes cannot break down easily. But in some cases bioremediation experts have found that they can use both aerobic and anaerobic bacteria to help with a tough cleanup job. (Aerobic bacteria need oxygen to survive and break down materials. Anaerobic bacteria, on the other hand, can function in an oxygen-free environment.)

General Electric Company, for example, is using both aerobic and anaerobic bacteria to attack waste that the company released into the Hudson River over a thirty-year period (1940 to 1970). The waste contains polychlorinated biphenyls (PCBs), chemicals that were once used in electrical equipment but are now outlawed because they are known carcinogens. PCB molecules are complex—no similar structures occur in nature—so bacteria have difficulty breaking them down. But in the early 1980s, GE researchers found anaerobic bacteria in the sediment of the Hudson River that were partially degrading PCBs. The problem now is to find ways to encourage the anaerobic bacteria on the floor of the river to multiply so that they can do their share of the cleanup work. Aerobic bacteria will be able to complete the job.

In experiments in South Carolina, scientists are developing a method for treating trichloroethylene (TCE), a cleaning solvent that causes cancer and has contaminated groundwater near the Savannah River nuclear weapons plant. Microbiologists discovered that a bacteria which could break down methane, another hazardous compound that had seeped into the water supply, could also decompose TCE. But the scientists were faced with a major problem. How could they encourage bacteria to grow in an aquifer, the area under ground where water is stored? They decided to use a bioreactor.

Basically, a bioreactor is a tank with filters. As water passes through the tank, bacteria adhere to the filters. To pump water through a bioreactor, two wells are drilled, one on each side of a contaminated area. Water is injected into one well and recovered from the other, which creates a flow of water.

In the TCE-cleansing process, which will take years to complete, bacteria that decompose the solvent are grown in the bioreactor, and then the contaminated groundwater is pumped through it. Eventually, biotechnologists on the project hope to inject TCE-eating bacteria directly into the aquifer along with a supply of methane to encourage their growth.

Another bioremediation experiment is being conducted at the Los Alamos Scientific Laboratory in New Mexico, where scientists are using microbes to decompose explosives. The bacteria were collected from sites around weapons plants where the soil was contaminated with such materials as TNT and nitroglycerin. Researchers then began raising more of the bacteria in the laboratory and found that several bacteria working in succession will decompose TNT. These bacteria may be effective in cleaning up hazardous wastes at munitions plants.

Researchers in laboratories across the United States, and around the world for that matter, are trying to identify bacteria that can be used to decompose many kinds of toxic wastes, including radioactive materials from nuclear weapons facilities and power plants. If these research efforts prove successful, bioremediation is expected to become an important industry in the years ahead.

7. Home Pest Management

The techniques of bioremediation, biotechnology, or biocontrol of pests may seem far removed from daily life. Most Americans give little thought to biological ways to manage waste or to control household, garden, and yard pests. When it comes to home pest control in particular, many people believe that the only effective strategy is using toxic chemicals. But the fact is that most of us can apply fairly simple biological techniques to control home, garden, and yard pests.

BIOCONTROL AT HOME

In recent years, dozens of books and magazine articles have included advice on how to use biological methods to control household pests. Some of this advice stems from research done by the staff at the Bio-Integral Resource Center (BIRC) in Berkeley, California. The nonprofit corporation includes a nationwide network of distinguished scientists, advisers, and researchers who have devised a wide variety of Integrated Pest Management methods to deal with pest problems throughout the United States and Canada.

Those who seek advice from BIRC include home owners, apartment managers, government agencies, pest control professionals, park directors, foresters, and farmers. They turn to the center for practical help in controlling a wide range of pests, from cockroaches and rodents in public and private buildings to fleas and ticks on pets to weeds and tree pests in urban areas. In its role as a key information center, BIRC publishes scientific studies on the least-toxic pest control measures and also *Common Sense Pest Control Quarterly* for the general public.

BIRC experts say that a beginning step in controlling household pests is to determine whether there is truly a problem. A few ants on a counter may not be a pest problem in the making. A squish or squash here and there may take care of a few "invaders," and further action may not be necessary.

Another preventive measure is cleaning up areas that attract pests. Experts suggest storing firewood and garbage cans away from living quarters and rinsing empty cans and bottles before throwing them away.

To keep pests out of homes, sealing cracks and other entryways helps. Electric zappers hung outdoors do away with flies, mosquitoes, and other pesky insects, but these devices have disadvantages—they may kill beneficial insects along with the flying pests.

What do biocontrol experts advise when pesky insects actually invade a home? Traps may be one method of control. Many types of traps can be used to capture ants, cockroaches, flies, and rodents. Such traps are available in garden shops, hardware stores, and supermarkets.

Homemade traps can capture fleas. If you put a desk lamp beside a solution of beer and dishwashing soap in a shallow pan, the heat and light from the lamp will attract fleas, which fall into the solution and die.

BIRC and others who advise on least-toxic pest control measures also suggest using biopesticides and similar products considered safe for the environment and human health. Here is just a sampling:

Boric acid in powder form effectively kills off ants and cockroaches. Some people mix it with sugar and sprinkle it under sinks and shelf paper, around refrigerators and stoves, at entry ways, in windowsills, and wherever the insects might enter a home. Others lay trails of boric acid around baseboards. However, pest control experts warn that boric acid may be toxic to household pets and young children, so it should be used with care.

Pyrethrum powders mixed with silica gel can be used for many pest insects including fleas on house pets. What is pyrethrum? It comes from the blossoms of a type of chrysanthemum flower and is used in pest control products.

Diatomaceous earth, called DE, is a biopesticide made up of the shells or skeletons of sea life called diatoms mined from the ocean. The remains are ground into a fine powder or crystals, which are so sharp that they cut through a soft-bodied insect's protective coating, causing it to lose body water and die. DE also dehydrates insect eggs. The powders are safe for household use and can be sprinkled in cupboards and other places where ants and roaches might hide. The biopesticide also destroys many garden pests, such as aphids, slugs, and thrips.

Another biological product controls rodents. It is Vitamin D3 in pellet form. Although the vitamin is a nutrient, rodents cannot process it. After rodents eat the pellets, calcium builds up in their blood, which causes death. Necessary Trading Company, a mail-order firm in

Virginia that sells organic products for farms and gardens, tested Vitamin D3 in its warehouse full of animal feed and other products rodents eat. The company says the product eliminated mice and rats without contaminating the remaining carcasses.

These and similar products may be available in some farm and garden stores, but most have to be ordered from mail-order companies that supply household, garden, and agricultural supplies considered safe for the environment. (Addresses for some of these companies are listed in Appendix 2.)

TRAUMA OVER TERMITES

Of all the pests that can infest a home, one that can bring out the worst in people is termites. They can turn docile folks into warriors, ready to reach for any kind of chemical that will kill. These insects can greatly damage buildings, eating away at foundations, porches, and walls. Some termites feed on dry wood; others (dampwood termites) feed on wood near leaking pipes or on damp, decaying porch or foundation timbers.

A termite's natural function is to help decompose dead wood, but nobody wants a termite infestation in her or his home, office, business, or other building.

For many years exterminators have used highly toxic pesticides to kill termites, but some exterminating companies, including well-known ones such as Orkin and Terminix, are offering alternative ways to destroy termites. One eradication method for drywood termites became available in 1990 from a California company called Isothermics. A University of California entomologist developed and patented the process, which involves heating a building to 150°F. The building is covered with a tent and hot air from propane heaters is pumped inside. Fans circulate the air for several hours until the temperature is high enough to kill the termites inside the wood.

Another method, called the Blizzard System, was developed by Tallon Termite and Pest Control company, also in California. The company has been using the system since 1985 for small areas of a building. Exterminators drill small holes in walls (which are later patched) and pump in liquid nitrogen, which drops the temperature to well below 0°F, freezing the termites to death.

Still another method utilizes an electrogun, a device that zaps termites with lethal doses of electricity. Pest control workers must first find termite tunnels in the soil or in wooden structures, then aim and shoot the gun accurately at their targets. If termites are zapped, their digestive systems break down and they die. Manufacturers of the electrogun recommend that only trained pest control workers use this method.

A few exterminators have used beneficial nematodes to successfully destroy termites in the soil. Even if pest control companies are not aware of this method, consumers can order beneficial nematodes from one of the mailorder companies supplying biopesticides, and the companies will provide instructions for professional application.

In some cases, termite infestations become so severe that the use of chemical pesticides may be the only way to clean up a building. Sometimes exterminators must fumigate a building by covering it with a huge tent and then pumping pesticides inside.

GARDENING WITH BIOCONTROLS

"When insects invade a treasured garden, many gardeners automatically will arm themselves for the 'battle with the bugs.' On go the masks and gloves; out come the . . . spray-guns and dusters," writes naturalist Craig Tufts whose column on gardening and backyard wildlife appears in many newspapers across the nation. Tufts, who holds a degree in environmental education from Cornell University, underscores the findings of a National Academy of Sciences study—home owners tend to use ten times more toxic chemicals per acre to control pests than growers use on agricultural cropland. (Tufts 1988)

But to keep their gardens chemical-free or to reduce their use of chemicals, some home gardeners, like some agricultural growers, are releasing "good bugs" to get rid of "bad bugs." Did you know, for example, that you can buy a carton of ladybugs to release in a garden? The adult beetles and the ladybug larvae devour aphids. Home gardeners also scatter lacewing larvae among their plants to control aphids, mealybugs, and red mites. And those tiny wasps, *Trichogramma*, can kill the eggs of moths that will eventually become pesky caterpillars or worms that chew on garden plants.

Other biocontrol measures include using pheromone traps and traps of bright yellow strips coated with a sticky material that captures small flying insects. Some gardeners build ponds or maintain areas of tall grasses to attract toads and frogs, which in turn snack on slugs, snails, and other pests that feed on vegetable plants.

Plant-eating worms and caterpillars can be eliminated with *Bt* powders that are dissolved in water to activate the bacteria that go after the pests. Other biopesticides for home gardens include insecticidal soaps sprayed on plants—rather like an old-fashioned tactic of dumping dishwater on gardens to control insects. Pyrethrins (similar to those used against indoor pests) and insecticides made with rotenone, an extract from plant roots, kill many insect pests.

Although all of these substances are relatively safe for wildlife, some can be toxic to honeybees and other beneficial insects. They also can harm fish, so they are not recommended for use on gardens near rivers and lakes; residues from the biopesticides could wash into the streams.

Another way that gardeners reduce the use of chemicals in a home garden is to mix and rotate the types of plants grown. Just as monoculture on farms tends to provide a habitat that allows pests to become established, so row after row of one kind of garden plant can invite pests. For example, rows of radishes may tempt some insects, but if a gardener plants one row of lettuce, then a row of radishes, and another in carrots, and so on, the insects tend to get confused and move on.

Organic growers also recommend repellent planting as one more way that insect pests can be controlled without chemical spraying. Many repellent plants have strong scents that fend off insect pests. *The Encyclopedia of Natural Insect & Disease Control*, compiled by researchers at the Rodale Farm, lists dozens of plants, including herbs, flowers that repel insects, and members of the onion family. Some examples: Garlic and chives repel aphids; marigolds, petunias, and the herb rosemary fend off Mexican bean beetles that attack snap beans; nasturtiums and marigolds repel whiteflies. The encyclopedia also includes recommendations for using various repellent plants to repulse larger animal pests such as mice, moles, and rabbits.

However, the Rodale researchers warn that "repellent plants may not perform consistently" and advise growers to experiment and observe carefully what goes on in their own gardens or orchards. By noting what types of plants pests avoid, growers can place these plants near crops that need protection. (Yepsen, Jr. 1984)

Sarah Slabaugh, a great-grandmother who spends most of her summer days in her herb and vegetable garden, has long been a patient observer of plants and pests. She notes: "I plant a lot of different herbs to keep pests from attacking my food plants. My tomato plants are free of pests with rue planted next to them. Tansy and mint plants are wonderful insect deterrents, too. I even planted some mint by my back door to control mosquitoes. They used to get in the house every time I opened the door, but I haven't noticed any with the mint nearby." (Personal interview, August 1990)

Still another method of pest control is making sure that plants are healthy. Plants grown in healthy soil tend to be stronger and better able to resist pests than plants grown in nutrient-poor soil. Some gardeners buy organic fertilizers (from natural products such as animal wastes and compost) to put nutrients in the soil. Other growers recycle yard waste, food scraps, and wood chips to make their own compost. Hundreds of recent articles and dozens of books provide advice on composting methods and equipment. Many students across the United States are learning about composting as they study recycling and other ways to protect the earth from a barrage of pollutants.

A CHEMICAL-FREE LAWN

Along with home gardeners who are kicking their chemical habits in growing crops, landowners and some landscaping professionals are rethinking their use of lawn chemicals. As many news articles have pointed out re-

Sarah Slabaugh of Milford, Indiana, shows off the rue she planted next to her tomatoes. She has experimented with companion planting—using certain plants to control insects that feed on food crops. "The rue has helped ward off pests that usually attack the tomatoes," she says. (Photo by the author.)

cently, songbirds and other wildlife are being poisoned by chemical insecticides sprayed on lawns. When insecticides are applied, earthworms come to the surface to escape the toxins. Birds quickly go for the worms, a tasty but lethal treat.

A few years ago, a New York wildlife pathologist performed autopsies on dead birds gathered from lawns and golf courses in the suburbs of the nation's capital. He found that the birds had died of pesticide poisoning. The birds' body tissue contained lethal levels of chlordane plus dieldrin and other toxic chemicals contained in lawn-care products, according to a report in the *Washington Post*. (Levy 1989)

Consumers Union, which tests and reports on many consumer products, surveyed home pesticide products in 1987 and found that some of the active ingredients commonly used on lawns caused cancer, birth defects, and damage to the nervous systems of laboratory animals. CU also noted that most ingredients in lawn-care products had not been tested for safety. "Even lawn-care giant ChemLawn notes in its literature that overexposure to various chemicals it applies can lead to headache, dizziness, blurred vision, chest pain, nausea, vomiting, and muscle weakness." ("The Green Way to a Green Lawn" 1990)

People do not have to use toxic chemicals to grow good lawns, writes Warren Schultz, author of *The Chemical-Free Lawn* and editor in chief of *National Gardening* Magazine. Schultz advises landowners and lawn-care professionals to think of a lawn as "a garden of grass" and to pull out weeds rather than use toxic herbicides. He writes: "If disease strikes, find out why and eliminate the cause. If insects move in, don't panic: Accept some damage and use safe biological controls when necessary." (Schultz 1990)

Some of the biocontrols used on gardens apply to lawns also. Many biopesticides for lawn care are available from garden and farm supply companies. *Bt* and predatory nematodes are common nonchemical options to use against insects.

The experts also emphasize that healthy lawns (like healthy garden plants) and nutrient-rich soil deter insect pests. To keep a lawn and soil fit does not mean applying heavy and frequent doses of fertilizer, however. New research shows that massive doses are not only wasteful of money but are harmful as well. Heavy fertilizer use reduces the ability of grass to make efficient use of nitrogen the natural way. If fertilizers have to be used, Schultz and other lawn-care experts say that organic fertilizers are best because they work slowly, releasing nutrients as needed.

Fertilizing may not be necessary at all if grass clippings are left on the lawn. The clippings are converted to nutrients used by the grass plants. In fact, if lawn mowing and bagging grass clippings is one of your regular chores (and you hate it), you could reduce your labor by following the advice of experts: "Cut it high and let it lie."

Some landowners who have decided to reduce their use of chemical fertilizers and pesticides have opted for lawns *without* grass. They plant ivy or other ground cover that needs little feeding and may resist many pests. In areas with little rainfall, gravel, wood chips, and such plants as cacti are part of the landscaping. Wildflowers and herb gardens sometimes take the place of lawns.

Encouraging birds to feed on insects in a lawn is another widely practiced alternative. Birds are usually attracted to lawns where there are shrubs with berries. Many people set up birdhouses and feeders to lure birds to their yards. Birds are, in fact, one of the many kinds of wildlife that can help with backyard pest control.

A tourist points out a purple-martin birdhouse that stands in a display area at a state park. Such birdhouses can encourage an increase in purple martins, birds that feed on insect pests. (Photo by the author.)

BACKYARD BIOAGENTS

Most people know that birds have an appetite for more than lawn insects. In fact, an oft-repeated historical event involves birds that saved crops in Utah. During the 1840s, Mormon settlers were plagued with hundreds of thousands of crickets that threatened to destroy their food supply. But flocks of gulls came from the Great Salt Lake to gobble up the crickets, wiping out the pests. Today, a monument honoring the sea gulls stands in the heart of Salt Lake City.

Many other birds prey on insect pests that attack trees. The busy woodpecker is an example. Perhaps you have heard the steady tap-tap-tap of a woodpecker searching for insects along a tree trunk. Scarlet tanagers, identified by their bright red bodies and black wings and tail, go after gypsy moths that attack trees in midwestern and eastern woodlands, parks, and backyards. The small acrobatic chickadee can hang upside down on a twig to capture insects on the tips or undersides of branches. Nuthatches, which also have some acrobatic abilities, can find insect larvae as they move headfirst down the trunk of a tree.

Along with birds, other kinds of animals help control backyard or garden pests. Large wasps known as paper wasps are among them. (They are called paper wasps because they build their nests of paperlike material made of wood and fiber pulp.) Not many people think of these wasps, which include hornets and yellowjackets, as beneficial predators. They can send many a home gardener, camper, fruit picker, or garbage worker running for cover. Indeed, it is sometimes necessary to spray these wasps with a chemical insecticide or risk being stung. But paper wasps like to prey on caterpillars, beetles, and other plant pests. They are also scavengers, cleaning up food scraps left by picnickers or feasting on uncovered garbage.

Spiders do their share of pest control work, too. These animals usually are called insects, but they are arachnids that many people label pests. In fact, spiders sometimes instill terror in people. Extreme fear of spiders, called arachnophobia, may stem from myths and distortions about these eight-legged creatures. Some of those distortions have been the basis for movies and TV shows. Even a well-known nursery rhyme depicts a spider as a threatening animal. Remember a frightened Miss Muffet who dropped her curds and whey all because a spider sat down beside her?

Most spiders control a variety of insect pests. Grass spiders spin silky funnel webs that spread over grass or soil. When insects are caught in the web, the spider, which has been hiding in the funnel, runs out and snatches its prey. (Photo by the author.)

Unfortunately, arachnophobes may not be aware of the spider's beneficial role as described in another nursery rhyme: "Come into my parlor, said the spider to the fly," indicating that the animal is setting an insect trap. Spiders spin silk webs in a variety of shapes and designs—bowls, triangles, platforms, domes, and complicated zigzagging bands—to capture insects. They control gnats, houseflies, roaches, mosquitoes, and many other pesky insects.

Most of the thousands of spider species are in fact a benefit to the environment and do not endanger humans, except for people who happen to be highly allergic to spider bites. Only three species are lethal: the black widow, the brown recluse, and the Australian funnel web spider. However, anyone who is bitten by a spider and experiences symptoms such as nausea, muscle cramps, and fever may be poisoned and should get immediate medical attention.

Contrary to popular views, tarantulas do not cause serious harm. Health officials warn, though, that if spiders—or other animals such as ticks or bees—bite, causing extreme pain or swelling, you should get medical help.

Bats also control great numbers of insects. The most common bat species in the United States can devour five hundred mosquitoes an hour. Within twenty-four to thirty-six hours, a bat will eat enough insects to equal its own body weight, consuming not only mosquitoes but also moths and beetles.

However, like spiders, bats have been the subject of mythical horror stories over the years. So frightening are bats to people that great numbers of these flying mammals have been killed. In some parts of the world, bats could become extinct. But an organization known as Bat Conservation International in Austin, Texas, is trying not only to save bats for their ecological benefits but also to debunk generally accepted myths about bats.

Even though you may have heard otherwise, bats in North America are *not* blind mice that fly. Bats do not get into your hair. They see very well and also have such sensitive sonar, or sound-wave, systems that they do not bump into people or things. In fact, scientists have used bats as models for sonar devices developed for the military and medical research. A bat's sonar helps it detect insects and determine whether they are edible.

Bats are commonly believed to transmit rabies, but rarely is this the case. Finally, to dispel one more myth: Bats are not vampires that suck blood from your neck. The only bats that suck blood live in Latin America, and they attack cows, not humans.

Of course, few people want bats living in their attic, and they may be concerned about bats that live in a nearby barn or cave. John Whitaker, Jr., an Indiana professor of life sciences and an expert on bats, receives hundreds of calls every year from people who want advice on getting rid of these mammals.

"Usually I try to explain that just having bats around is not dangerous, but if people cannot tolerate these animals, then controlling them does not mean killing them. More bats will just take their place. But a person can put screen, boards, nets, or other materials over places where bats enter a home or other building," Whitaker says. (Phone interview and correspondence, August 1990)

PESKY MAMMALS

Along with bats, other kinds of animals make their way into people's yards and sometimes become intolerable. Moles, rats, gophers, rabbits, squirrels, and raccoons are

A state park naturalist shows the underside of a bat house. Bats attach themselves to the dividers in the house. Such structures are set up to provide safe havens for bats, animals that feed on and control many kinds of insects, including mosquitoes. (Photo by the author.)

some mammals that can be pests. Such animals may be more destructive than helpful to people and their property. They may invade backyards looking for food because home and road construction and other urban expansion have forced the animals from their natural habitats.

Can people protect their property from such pests without using poisons? The answer is yes, but the methods vary considerably. Generally, though, most nonpoisonous pest controls are traps or protective barriers placed around garden plants, shrubs, and trees. Growers can make their own animal traps or buy them from garden shops, hardware stores, or mail-order firms.

Some gardeners opt to create a backyard haven for animals. You can find information on the subject in books such as Craig Tufts's *The Backyard Naturalist*, published by the National Wildlife Federation. Organic gardening books and magazines and environmental magazines also cover the topic.

8. Learning to Protect the Earth

Just north of Tucson, Arizona, an unusual experiment is focusing on how the Earth, a self-contained system, supports life. The experiment, sponsored by a private company, is taking place inside a complex of buildings that looks like a series of greenhouses. Years in the making, the gigantic glassed-in modules dubbed Biosphere II cover an area the size of three football fields. The complex is a self-sustaining ecosystem modeled after Biosphere I (Earth) and includes a farm, marsh, desert, ocean, savannah, and rain forest, complete with animals and plants. There are also living quarters for eight scientists.

Organic agriculture is a necessary part of the experiment, since any chemicals would circulate through the closed system, moving from the farm to the breakfast table within a few days. Researchers are using such agricultural methods as planting disease-resistant crops, mixing the types of plants to be grown, and rotating crops on their farm. Natural pest control is a must, and beneficial insects are bred in one of the many support buildings outside Biosphere II. Other buildings surrounding the biosphere hold monitoring systems and communication facilities so that researchers can keep in touch with the outside world via computers, telephones, video, and other electronic equipment.

Biologists and agricultural experts have created as diverse an ecosystem as possible, bringing in plants and animals from around the world. But they do not know what imbalances might occur. Perhaps a species of insect or microbe could multiply rapidly and get out of control. Maybe a colony of bats that live in a cave will not find enough insects to survive. The mix of microbes in the soil or "ocean" might create havoc with their ecological systems. But as researchers study the systems inside Biosphere II, they hope to gain some knowledge about what it takes to maintain ecological balances on the planet.

NEEDED CHANGES

Although Biosphere II seems to be a far-out experiment, it may call public attention to the need to understand Earth's biological systems. Perhaps the experiment will foster more interest in the use of biological methods to clean up waste, or will prompt more support for alternative agriculture and biological pest control.

Whatever the results of the experiment, many more efforts will be needed to bring about significant reductions in the production and use of agrichemicals and chemical products for home gardens and yards and recreation areas. For one thing, federal policies will have to be changed to encourage widespread adoption of natural farming methods. Increased funding for research and incentives to encourage alternative agriculture also are needed. Public education will be necessary as well, since many people believe that natural farming methods are a return to "primitive" agriculture and reflect an antitechnology stance. That view was expressed in an editorial published in *The Elkhart Truth*, a newspaper serving a midsize Indiana city in the heart of America's farm belt:

> *They're Ba-ack. The same folks who brought us the Alar scare, or their close kin, are back again, this time organized under the thoroughly frightening title "National Toxics Campaign" and working to make us scared of virtually every carrot and asparagus stalk in the store. . . .*
>
> *The toxic campaigners are playing up that effect by creating fear that pesticides may be a danger to health. The ordinary consumer doesn't have any way to evaluate these claims. . . .*
>
> *How distressed would be previous generations who worked long and hard to get into place the system we have. Seeing food shortages and needless spoilage, they struggled to get science in food production treated in a rational way; now there are people who want to dump that overboard in favor of emotional responses. ("Horror in the Produce Aisles" 1989)*

The editorial concluded that a campaign against pesticide residues on food supplies was done to "satisfy someone's emotional need for a more primitive sense of the world" so "ought to be rejected."

CITIZEN ACTION

In spite of such views, a growing number of citizens have responded to reports from agricultural experts who have expressed concerns about the harmful effects of toxic pesticides and other hazardous chemicals. Many citizens across the United States have become active in groups such as the National Toxics Campaign, the National Coalition Against Misuse of Pesticides, and the Natural Resources Defense Council. Others have joined broad-based environmental organizations such as the National Audubon Society, the National Wildlife Federation, the Sierra Club, and Greenpeace.

One area of chemical use that prompts community activism is the commercial application of pesticides and fertilizers by lawn-care companies. Although a few lawn-care companies use biocontrol methods, most commercial companies such as ChemLawn and Tru Green rely on

In many cities and towns, citizens form action groups to educate people about hazardous materials, which include many synthetic chemical pesticides. Action groups also set up community hazardous waste collection sites so that people can bring their hazardous materials to the sites for safe disposal. (Photo by the author.)

chemicals to attack pests. Companies say that the chemicals in the mixtures they use are greatly diluted and that a sprayed area is safe within a few hours. But more and more consumers are objecting to chemical sprays.

In the Philadelphia area, for example, several mothers collected a hundred signatures on a petition to convince their local school board that chemical pesticides should not be sprayed on school property. As one mother put it: "If the chemicals can kill bugs and weeds for a month, they can hurt my kid for a month." (Peck 1990)

Legislators in some cities across the nation and about a dozen states have passed "right-to-know" laws that require lawn-care companies to post signs notifying residents of chemical spraying. Some legislation also requires companies to keep records of the types of chemicals used on customers' lawns. Companies have protested such laws because of the paperwork involved, the costs of the signs, and the fact that some home owners remove the signs minutes after they have been put up. Yet proponents say that residents in a neighborhood, especially those sensitive or allergic to chemicals, have the right to know what is being sprayed on lawns and when applications take place.

A few years ago along the eastern seaboard, similar protests raged over spraying of herbicides on wooded areas to control the gypsy moth. State agencies offered two choices for insecticides—the bacterial preparation Bt or a synthetic chemical called Dimilin. Most people opted for Dimilin, believing that it was the more effective pest control product.

Since Dimilin can destroy beneficial insects as well as other animals, citizen groups pressured government agencies to offer residents a choice. Residents could either refuse any type of spraying on their property or decide which type of spraying they would accept. As a result, in some states only *Bt* applications are being used. In one Connecticut community that decided not to spray at all, trees have been harmed less than in neighboring towns. Apparently, some natural enemies of the gypsy moth have been able to prey on the pests.

Some community action projects also have been initiated to protest aerial spraying of pesticides on agricultural crops, since these chemicals often drift onto private property and may endanger people in a spray area. In Southern California, for example, community groups have adamantly protested spraying of malathion used to control Mediterranean fruit flies, which feed on oranges and other fruits. The female Medfly, as it is called, is a particularly dangerous pest because it attacks the fruit, not the plant, laying eggs directly into an orange. When the eggs hatch, the maggots munch away inside the fruit, frequently leaving it unsuitable for human consumption.

When the Medfly infested northern California orchards between 1981 and 1982, biocontrol was the first line of defense. Male Medflies were bred in large quantities in the laboratory and sterilized by radiation, then released into an infested area. Females that mated with the sterile males laid eggs that did not hatch. But unfortunately an accident occurred. Thousands of the Medflies released by the USDA had been mislabeled and turned out to be fertile, which increased the infestation. Citrus growers and some political leaders pressured for aerial spraying of malathion insecticide, which medical and government officials said was nontoxic to humans and pets. Nearly 1,500 square miles were sprayed time after time with the insecticide.

During 1989 to 1990, the Medfly again infested California but was concentrated in southern counties. State officials immediately began releasing sterile male Medflies. But the insectary breeding the flies could not keep up with the demand for millions of insects, so the malathion spraying was initiated and went on for months. Many Southern California residents protested angrily, expressing fears about health hazards of the insecticide and demanding a stop to the aerial spraying. Some toxicologists also noted their concerns about the toxic effects of the insecticide. In early 1990, the *Los Angeles Times* polled 1,900 residents whose neighborhoods had been sprayed and found that one out of every five people suffered from health problems blamed on the pesticide spraying. (Decker 1990)

The debate over the safety of malathion has yet to be settled. But state officials believe that their spraying successfully eliminated the Medfly infestation. The supply of sterile Medflies is expected to be large enough to control any new Medfly infestations without spraying malathion repeatedly.

Some community action groups have worked with local government agencies to combat mosquito infestations the least toxic way. For many years, chemical pesticides seemed to be the only way to kill mosquitoes, which are more than just a nuisance; they also spread deadly diseases. But as with other insects, mosquitoes have been able to survive chemical insecticides and strains have developed that are resistant to chemical sprays.

Although chemicals may be needed in some instances to curb serious infestations of disease-carrying mosquitoes, both private and public groups have consulted with biocontrol experts such as those at BIRC. Most recommend using *Bt* insecticides whenever possible to control mosquitoes. These insecticides can be sprayed on breeding sites in parks, on croplands, or in backyards.

Another biocontrol measure is stocking waterways with

mosquito-eating fish. Since many species of mosquitoes breed in standing water, marshes, and other wet areas, researchers are attempting to identify fish that can be introduced into a specific habitat without disrupting that ecosystem.

GETTING IN TOUCH WITH NATURE

Whether or not you become part of a community action group, you can still take an active role in learning more about the beneficial organisms that may be in your own backyard or nearby vacant lot or park. For years, such organizations as the Sierra Club, the National Audubon Society, and the National Wildlife Federation and youth groups like the Girl Scouts, Boy Scouts, and 4H have sponsored programs that help young people, as well as adults, get hands-on experience with environmental projects. Many schools also are offering classes or projects that provide opportunities to learn about the environment. Students may study and take care of a plot of land next to the school, learning about the living organisms that keep the land productive and in balance.

Even very young children get involved in tending to the land. In Costa Mesa, California, employees at a day care center on the campus of Orange Coast College help youngsters care for a garden a few blocks away. Most of the children in the day care center live in nearby apartments or condominiums and seldom if ever have a chance to observe how plants grow or where food comes from. A geology professor at the college came up with the idea for a children's garden, which the day care youngsters plant with such vegetables as beans, squash, tomatoes, and corn. Armed with small hoes, the children weed and till the plot and also water the plants as needed. Teachers help the

Some students are able to visit a nature center, where they can learn more about insects and other animals that inhabit the earth. Here students inspect a tarantula and learn that the spider is harmless and furry-soft to the touch. (Photo by the author.)

Caring for a vegetable patch is one way to get in touch with the earth. (Photo by Betterae McIntyre-Gay.)

youngsters identify beneficial insects—ladybugs are favorites—which feed on pests in their garden. Through their gardening activities, kids gain a sense of responsibility for tending to the earth and recognize that the real source of their food supply is the land not the supermarket.

Adults, too, frequently need to be reminded where food and fiber come from, and displays showing diverse aspects of agriculture traditionally have been part of county fairs. However, as the number of people needed to produce agricultural goods has steadily declined, many Americans have little contact with the land. As a result, their life-styles frequently clash with those of the farm community. Nowhere is this more apparent than in rural areas where some farmland has given way to housing developments and shopping centers.

When communities are built next to farms, some suburbanites have shown little tolerance for the ordinary activities of farming. In a community west of Chicago, for example, a suburban resident sued a farmer for running his tractor at night, a common practice during planting and harvesting. The farmer was accused of violating a noise ordinance. Although the suit was eventually dropped, the court case demonstrates the need for understanding what goes on in farming.

Similar conflicts have troubled Maryland counties where urban sprawl has taken over much farmland. Suburbanites complain about not only tractor noise but also slow-moving farm equipment that must travel the roads to get from one field to another. In addition, people object to the odor of manure that drifts over the area when fields are fertilized. To counteract these complaints and to provide public education about agriculture, several counties have constructed farm centers that bring together experts to aid farmers in addition to offering educational programs for school children studying the environment. Such a facility also is a place where residents can learn about composting and pest control for home gardens.

Even if you do not have the opportunity to get involved in a school or community environmental project, you can learn about the earth and some of its beneficial organisms on your own. Libraries, for example, have plenty of books and magazine articles on plants and insects, arachnids, bats, and other biocontrol agents.

You might gain some firsthand experiences by taking part in such activities as building a bird feeder or bat house to create a safe haven for these insect eaters. You can start your own insect collection or use an environmental chemistry set to analyze drinking water and soil. You can find materials for some of these projects at garden shops, bookstores, and mail-order supply companies that sell environmentally safe products. Biologists, conservationists, and naturalists at state and national parks also can be a help in suggesting ways to learn about how the natural world works.

The more each of us learns about the specific roles that species of plants and animals play, (whether it's the "good bugs" that control the "bad bugs" or bacteria that gobble up waste), the more we can learn to appreciate the interdependence of all living things. As William Reilly, administrator of the EPA and former head of the Conservation Foundation, noted on Earth Day 1990:

Our planet's natural systems do not exist just to be exploited or to support human economic activity. Nature has an intrinsic worth that . . . should be respected. We should all take responsibility for . . . nurturing and sustaining the planet that nurtures and sustains us. (Reilly 1990)

Appendix 1

ORGANIZATIONS

Agricultural Research Service
U.S. Department of
   Agriculture
Room 318, B-005, BARC-West
Beltsville, MD 20705

Bio-Integral Resource Center
P.O. Box 7414
Berkeley, CA 94707

Environmental Defense Fund
257 Park Avenue South
New York, NY 10010

Friends of the Earth
218 D Street SE
Washington, D.C. 20003

Greenpeace
1436 U Street NW
Washington, D.C. 20009

Industrial Biotechnology
   Association
1625 K Street NW
Suite 1100
Washington, D.C. 20006-1604

National Audubon Society
950 Third Avenue
New York, NY 10022

National Wildlife Federation
1400 16th Street NW
Washington, D.C. 20036-2266

Sierra Club
730 Polk Street
San Francisco, CA 94109

Soil Conservation Service
U.S. Department of
   Agriculture
Room 5105, South Building
Washington, D.C. 20250

The Wilderness Society
1400 Eye Street NW
Washington, D.C. 20005

World Wildlife Fund
1250 24th Street NW
Washington, D.C. 20037

Worldwatch Institute
1776 Massachusetts Avenue
   NW
Washington, D.C. 20036

Appendix 2

SUPPLIERS OF BIOCONTROL PRODUCTS

Beneficial Biosystems
P.O. Box 8461
Emeryville, CA 94662

Biofac
P.O. Box 87
Mathis, TX 78368

Garden Supply
128 Intervale Road
Burlington, VT 05401

Gardens Alive!
P.O. Box 149
Sunman, IN 47041

Growing Naturally
149 Pine Lane
P.O. Box 54
Pineville, PA 18946

Harmony Farm Supply
P.O. Box 460
Graton, CA 95444

Nature's Touch
11150 Addison Street
Franklin Park, IL 60131

Necessary Trading Company
New Castle, VA 24127

Peaceful Valley Farm Supply
P.O. Box 2209
Grass Valley, CA 95945

Pest Management Supply
   Company
P.O. Box 938
Amherst, MA 01004

Rincon-Vitova Insectaries
P.O. Box 95
Oak View, CA 93022

Ringer
9959 Valley View Road
Eden Prairie, MN 55344-3585

Safer, Inc.
189 Wells Avenue
Newton, MA 02159

Seventh Generation
10 Farrell Street
South Burlington, VT 05403

Glossary

Aerobic: requiring oxygen to live.

Agrichemicals: chemical products used in agriculture, such as fertilizers and pesticides.

Anaerobic: living in the absence of oxygen.

Antibiotic: a substance used to treat bacterial infections.

Aquatic: living in water or adapted to water.

Aquifer: a geologic formation where water saturates the earth.

Arachnid: a class of animals that includes the spider, mite, and tick.

ARS: Agricultural Research Service.

Bacterium: a single-celled organism (plural: bacteria).

Bioagent: a term to describe organisms that destroy animal and plant pests.

Biocontrol: a short form of the term biological control.

Biological control: a method for using biological organisms to reduce or destroy harmful insects and other organisms.

Biomass: all of the biological matter in a specific area.

Bioremediation: a process in which bacteria and fungi feed on various pollutants in water and soil.

Biotechnology: using a biological process to develop products or to alter products.

Carcinogen: a cancer-causing substance.

Cell: the basic unit of life, which may exist independently or combine with other cells to form colonies or tissues.

Compost: plant and vegetable matter that decay and can be used as fertilizer.

DNA: deoxyribonucleic acid, the molecule in cells that carries the instructions, or genes, that control hereditary traits.

Ecology: the study of how living things relate to their environment.

Entomologist: a person who studies insects.

Enzyme: a substance in a cell that brings about chemical reactions or changes.

EPA: Environmental Protection Agency.

FDA: Food and Drug Administration.

Fungicide: a type of pesticide that kills fungi.

Fungus: plantlike organism; fungi (plural) make up one of the classifications of living things.

Gene: a cell particle that controls heredity.

Groundwater: water below the earth's surface.

Herbicide: a type of pesticide that kills plants that are pests, such as weeds.

Hybrid: offspring of two plants or animals of different species or varieties.

Insecticide: a type of pesticide that kills insects.

Insects: a varied group of small six-legged animals that usually have segmented bodies, antennae, and wings.

IPM: Integrated Pest Management.

Larva: an insect in its wormlike stage (plural: larvae).

Mammal: member of the Mammalia class of animals; includes females that produce milk.

Microorganism (also **microbe**): any organism that is so small it can be seen only with a microscope.

Nematode: microscopic soil worm.

Organic (in agriculture and gardening): refers to plants and animals free of synthetic chemicals.

Organic (in chemistry): made up of carbon compounds.

Parasite: an organism that lives on or inside plants or animals.

Pathogen: a disease-causing agent, such as a fungus, virus, or bacterium.

Pathologist: a person who studies plant and animal diseases.

Pesticides: a variety of chemical products that kill pests.

Pheromone: chemical substances that animals secrete.

Predator: an animal that lives by preying or feeding on others.

Rodenticide: a type of pesticide that kills rodents.

Technology: tools and techniques used to accomplish a purpose, such as to make products.

Toxicologist: a person who studies poisons and its effects.

Toxin: a poison.

USDA: United States Department of Agriculture.

Virus: a microscopic pathogen made up of genetic materials and protein that cannot survive outside of living cells but is capable of reproducing itself and causing disease.

Bibliography

Books and Booklets

Agricultural Research Service. *Agricultural Research.* Washington, D.C.: United States Department of Agriculture, March 1989.
———. *Research Progress in 1989.* Washington, D.C.: United States Department of Agriculture, June 1990.
———. *Solving Agricultural Problems With Biotechnology.* Washington, D.C.: United States Department of Agriculture, January 1990.
Animal and Plant Health Inspection Service. *Biological Control.* Washington, D.C.: United States Department of Agriculture, July 1987.
Berenbaum, May R. *Ninety-nine Gnats, Nits, and Nibblers.* Urbana and Chicago: University of Illinois Press, 1989.
Board on Agriculture of the National Research Council. *Alternative Agriculture.* Washington, D.C.: National Academy Press, 1989, pp. 8, 23, 121–125, 175.
Calder, Nigel. *The Green Machines.* New York: G. P. Putnam's Sons, 1989.
Danks, H.V. *The Bug Book.* New York: Workman Publishers, 1987.
Earth Works Group, The. *50 Simple Things You Can Do To Save The Earth.* Berkeley, California: Earthworks Press, 1989.
Edwards, Gabrielle I. *Biology the Easy Way* 2d. ed. New York: Barron's Educational Series, Inc., 1990.

Evans, Howard E. *The Pleasures of Entomology*, Washington, D.C.: Smithsonian Institution Press, 1985.

Garland, Anne Witte and the Natural Resources Defense Council. *For Our Kids' Sake: How to Protect Your Child Against Pesticides in Food*, San Francisco: Sierra Club Books, 1989.

Gay, Kathlyn. *Silent Killers*. New York: Franklin Watts, 1988.

———. *Water Pollution*. New York: Franklin Watts, 1990.

Graham, Ada, and Frank Graham. *Bug Hunters*. New York: Delacorte Press, 1978.

———. *Busy Bugs*. New York: Dodd, Mead, 1983.

Industrial Biotechnology Association. *Agriculture and the New Biology*. Washington, D.C.: Industrial Biotechnology Association, 1989.

———. *Answers to Commonly Asked Questions About Biotechnology Regulation*. (undated booklet)

———. *Biotechnology at Work*. Washington, D.C.: Industrial Biotechnology Association, 1989.

———. *What Is Biotechnology?* Washington, D.C.: Industrial Biotechnology Association, 1989.

Johnson, Sylvia A. *Bats*. Minneapolis, Minnesota: Lerner Books, 1985.

Milne, Margery and Lorus. *The Audubon Society Field Guide to North American Insects and Spiders*. New York: Alfred A. Knopf, 1980.

Mound, L. A. *Insects*. New York: Knopf, 1990.

Office of Technology Assessment, U.S. Congress. *Field-Testing Engineered Organisms: Genetic and Ecological Issues*. Washington, D.C.: Government Printing Office, 1988.

O'Toole, Christopher. *The Encyclopedia of Insects*. New York: Facts on File, 1986.

Parker, Nancy Winslow, and Joan Richards Wright. *Bugs*. New York: Greenwillow Books, 1987.

Philbrick, Helen and John. *The Bug Book: Harmless Insect Controls*. Charlotte, Vermont: Garden Way Publishers, 1974.

Schultz, Warren. *The Chemical Free Lawn*. Emmaus, Pennsylvania: Rodale Press, 1989.

Seymour, John, and Herbert Girardet. *Blueprint For a Green Planet*. New York: Prentice Hall/Simon & Schuster, 1987.

Smith, Miranda, and Anna Carr. *Rodale's Garden Insect, Disease & Weed Identification Guide*. Emmaus, PA: Rodale Press, 1988.

Stokes, Donald W. *A Guide to Observing Insects Lives*. Boston: Little, Brown, 1983.

Swan, Lester A. *Beneficial Insects*. New York: Harper and Row, 1964.

Tufts, Craig. *The Backyard Naturalist*. Washington, D.C.: National Wildlife Federation, 1988.

Tuttle, Merlin D. *America's Neighborhood Bats*. Austin, Texas: University of Texas Press, 1988.

Wild, Russell, ed. *The Earth Care Annual 1991*. Emmaus, Pennsylvania: Rodale Press, 1991.

Yepsen, Roger B., Jr. *The Encyclopedia of Natural Insect and Disease Control*. Emmaus, Pennsylvania: Rodale Press, 1984.

Periodicals

"Agriculture and the Environment." *EPA Journal*, April 1988 (entire issue).

"Bad Apples." *Consumer Reports*, May 1989, pp. 288–296.

Barnett, Robert. "Florida: Big Growers Cut Chemicals." *American Health*, July–August 1990, pp. 43–46.

Bass, Thomas A. "Africa's Drive to Win the Battle Against Insects." *Smithsonian*, August 1988, pp. 78–88.

Beck, Melinda, et al. "Warning! Your Food, Nutritious and Delicious, May Be Hazardous to Your Health." *Newsweek*, March 27, 1989.

Begley, Sharon, with Mary Hager and Judy Howard. "Dangers in the Vegetable Patch." *Newsweek*, January 30, 1989.

Best, Cheryl. "Natural Pest Controls." *Garbage*, September–October 1989, pp. 40–49.

Brookes, Warren T. "The Wasteful Pursuit of Zero Risk." *Forbes*, April 30, 1990, pp. 161–172.

Chinnici, Madeline. "Terror at the Table." *Discover*, January 1990, p. 74.

Chollar, Susan. "The Poison Eaters." *Discover*, April 1990, pp. 76–78.

Conniff, Richard. "You Never Know What the Fire Ant Is Going to Do Next." *Smithsonian*, July 1990, pp. 48–57.

Cowley, Geoffrey, with Rebecca Crandall. "Bad Water, Faulty Genes." *Newsweek*, September 3, 1990, p. 73.

Crawford, Mark. "Biotech Companies Lobby for Federal Regulation." *Science*, May 4, 1990, pp. 546–547.

Crosson, Pierre R., and Norman J. Rosenberg. "Strategies for Agriculture." *Scientific American*, September 1989, pp. 128–136.

Crowley, Patrice. "Our Over-Reliance on Pesticides." *Country Journal*, November–December 1989, p. 15.

"Cultivating Weeds for Pest Control." *Science News*, August 11, 1990, p. 93.

Davis, Bernard, and Lissa Roche. "Genetic Engineering: Sorcerer's Apprentice or Handmaiden to Humanity?" *USA Today*, November 1989, pp. 68–70.

Debus, Keith H. "Mining with Microbes." *Technology Review*, August–September 1990, pp. 50–57.

Decker, Cathleen. "Moratorium on Malathion Spraying Is Widely Backed." *Los Angeles Times*, February 11, 1990, p. A1.

Dibner, Mark D. "Factories of Our Future." *Consumers' Research*, April 1989, pp. 15–18.

Eikermann, Leland. "Why We Need More Sustainable Agriculture Research." *Citizens Power*, Summer 1990, p. 7.

"Explosive Bacteria." *Discover*, October 1989, p. 18.

Farley, Dixie. "Setting Safe Limits on Pesticide Residues." *FDA Consumer*, October 1988, pp. 8–11.

Ferrell, J. E. "The 100% Solution." *LA Times Magazine*, May 28, 1989, pp. 25–26.

Fritz, Michael. "Thank You, Jeremy Rifkin." *Forbes*, October 16, 1989, pp. 268–269.

Gillette, Becky. "Controlling Mosquitoes Biologically." *BioScience*, February 1988, pp. 80–83.

Goldsmith, Marsha F. "As Farmworkers Help Keep America Healthy, Illness May Be Their Harvest." *The Journal of the American Medical Association*, June 9, 1989, pp. 3207–3209.

"The Green Way to a Green Lawn." *Consumer Reports*, June 1990, pp. 399–402.

Gunset, George. " 'Sustainable' Crop Tests Get Good Grades." *Chicago Tribune*, January 29, 1990, p. 3.

Hof, Robert D. "The Tiniest Toxic Avengers." *Business Week*, June 4, 1990, pp. 96–98.

Holing, Dwight. "Looking for Mr. Goodbug." *Sierra*, January–February 1990, pp. 20–24.

Holmberg, Mike. "Pesticide Safety Is on the Minds of Farmers, Too." *Successful Farming*, September 1989, p. 4.

"Horror in the Produce Aisles." *The Elkhart Truth,* September 12, 1989, p. A4.

Huang, H. T., and Pei Yang. "The Ancient Cultured Citrus Ant." *BioScience,* October 1987, pp. 665–671.

Kourik, Robert. "Controlling Pests Without Chemical Warfare." *Garbage,* March–April 1990, pp. 22–29.

Krimsky, Sheldon, et al. "Controlling Risk in Biotech." *Technology Review,* July 1989, pp. 62–70.

Leahy, Patrick J. "Toward a National Biotechnology Policy." *Issues in Science and Technology,* Fall 1988, pp. 26–29.

Levy, Claudia. "Pretty Lawns May Be Lethal for Songbirds." *The Washington Post,* July 23, 1989, p. B1.

"Managing Pesticide Resistance." *BioScience,* April 1985, p. 217.

Manuel, John. "North Carolina Regulates Biotech." *Technology Review,* July 1990, pp. 20–21.

Marinelli, Janet. "Composting. From Backyards to Big-Time." *Garbage,* July–August 1990, pp. 44–50.

McDermott, Jeanne. "Some Heartland Farmers Just Say No to Chemicals." *Smithsonian,* April 1990, pp. 114–127.

McGuire, Richard. "Biotechnology and Agriculture." *Vital Speeches of the Day,* December 15, 1989, pp. 147–150.

Miller, Dale A. "The Biological Future of Pest Control." *Vital Speeches of the Day,* March 15, 1989, pp. 337–340.

Miller, Henry I., and Stephen J. Ackerman. "Perspective on Food Biotechnology." *FDA Consumer,* March 1990, pp. 8–13.

North Carolina Biotechnology Center. "North Carolina's Genetically Engineered Organisms Act." (news release, September 1989).

O'Connor, John. "Stop the Poisons at the Source." *Philadelphia Inquirer,* April 19, 1990, p. A23.

Olkowski, William, and Helga Olkowski. "Ants in the House." *Common Sense Pest Control Quarterly*, Spring 1990, p. 6.

Peck, Michael. "Spraying at School Raises Questions About Chemicals." *Philadelphia Inquirer*, May 2, 1990, p. G10.

Pimentel, David, and Lois Levitan. "Pesticides: Amounts Applied and Amounts Reaching Pests." *BioScience*, February 1986, pp. 86–91.

Reganold, John P., Robert I. Papendick, and James F. Parr. "Sustainable Agriculture." *Scientific American*, June 1990, pp. 112–120.

Reilly, William K. "A World in Our Hands." *Washington Post*, April 22, 1990, p. B1.

Reynolds, Larry. "But Where Will I Play Golf?" *Management Review*, June 1990, p. 15.

Ritter, Donald L., "Unshackle Scientists from Stifling Government Regulations," *USA TODAY*, November 1989, pp. 66–67.

Roberts, Leslie. "Pesticides and Kids." *Science*, March 10, 1989, pp. 1280–1281.

Rodale, Robert. "A New Garden Era." *Organic Gardening*, September 1989, p. 23.

Samuelson, Robert J. "The Absurd Farm Bill." *Newsweek*, August 6, 1990, p. 51.

Sanchez, Doris. "Blunting the Peachtree Borer." *Agricultural Research*, March 1989, p. 15.

Sattaur, Omar. "A New Crop of Pest Controls." *New Scientist*, July 14, 1988, pp. 48–54.

Schultz, Warren. "Natural Lawn Care." *Garbage*, July–August 1990, pp. 28–34.

Schwab, Jim. "The Attraction Is Chemical." *Nation*, October 16, 1989, p. 416–420.

Sheets, Kenneth R. "America's Giant Food Fight." *U.S. News & World Report*, April 30, 1990, pp. 39–42.

Sheets, Kenneth R., with William J. Cook and Betsy Carpenter. "Nature Vs. Nurture on the Farm." *U.S. News & World Report*, September 18, 1989, pp. 53–54.

Smith, Emily T., Meg Campbell, Richard Brandt, and Vicky Cahan. "Farmers Are Learning New Tricks from Mother Nature." *Business Week*, November 6, 1989, pp. 76–80.

Soviero, Marcelle M. "Bacteria That Eat TNT." *Popular Science*, November 1989, p. 116.

Stalcup, Larry. "Good Bugs Take a Bit Out of Stored Grain Pests." *Farm Journal*, August 1990, pp. 28–29.

Stiak, Jim. "The Pesticide Watch: What the Tests Don't Tell Us." *Horticulture*, December 1989, p. 16–18.

Thayer, Ann M. "Mycogen Poised to Launch New Generation of Biopesticides." *Chemical and Engineering News*, April 30, 1990.

———. "Sandoz Crop Protection Prepares for Changing Agrochemicals Industry." *Chemical and Engineering News*, August 6, 1990, pp. 15–17.

Tonge, Peter W. "The No-Pesticide Revolution." *World Monitor*, June 1989, pp. 56–60.

"Too Much Fuss About Pesticides?" *Consumer Reports*, October 1989, pp. 655–658.

Treakle, Kay, and John Sacko. "Attack of the Killer Bugs." *Greenpeace*, March–April 1989, pp. 12–13.

Van, Jon. "Professor Out to Oil-Proof Beaches." *Chicago Tribune*, June 14, 1990, p. 1.

Vaughan, Christopher. "Disarming Farming's Chemical Warriors." *Science News*, August 20, 1988, pp. 120–121.

Whelan, Elizabeth. "The Era of Rotten Apples." *Successful Farming*, February 15, 1990, p. 30.

Whitaker, Jr., John. "The Truth About Bats." *Outdoor Indiana*, May 1988, pp. 30–35.

"Yard Work." *New Age Journal*, March–April 1990, p. 65.

"Zapping Pests, Conscientiously." *U.S. News & World Report*, May 7, 1990, p. 77.

Index